Reverend

Reverend

*How Generation X Ministers Are
Shaping Unitarian Universalism*

EDITED BY
TAMARA LEBAK & BRET LORTIE

FOREWORD BY
MARLIN LAVANHAR

JENKIN LLOYD JONES PRESS
AT ALL SOULS UNITARIAN CHURCH
TULSA, OKLAHOMA

JENKIN LLOYD JONES PRESS
at All Souls Unitarian Church
2952 South Peoria
Tulsa, OK 74114
918-743-2363

Manuscript Editor: Sheri Reda
Copy Editor: Jean Caffey Lyles
Cover Art: Laurel Williamson
Design and production: Carl Brune

ISBN 978-0-9755389-2-0

To the movement.

CONTENTS

FOREWORD

I will never forget the adults' reaction to a youth worship service I participated in at a Unitarian Universalist summer camp many years ago. The older UUs were incensed that their teenagers were talking about faith, God, spirit, destiny, and prayer. "I thought our tradition was based in reason—what's happened?" one elderly man roared. The adults were perplexed by the theologies and practices of the young people of a new generation that was becoming known by the moniker "X." As young UUs in the 1980s, we were longing for spiritual practices to broaden our faith, and for religious experiences that moved us at least as much as the music we loved. Neither of these longings was being fulfilled in the sanctuaries of our home congregations.

Today, some of those teenagers of the '80s are UU ministers who lead worship in the same sanctuaries that once disappointed but also shaped them. The "X" in Generation X may ultimately signify a crossroad. In the scope of this collection you will discover imaginative new ways of envisioning the future along with many effective practices emerging from some of our most dynamic congregations.

Reverend X is by far the most provocative and important book published by Jenkin Lloyd Jones Press to date. It rethinks UU principles, practices, and cultural privileges in ways that articulate an underlying re-formation of our faith.

THE REV. MARLIN LAVANHAR
Senior Minister
All Souls Church, Tulsa, Oklahoma
Publisher
Jenkin Lloyd Jones Press

INTRODUCTION

Who are Generation X ministers? If nothing else, we are the "third wave" of ministers coming online since the Unitarians and the Universalists merged in 1961. The first wave brought the two denominations together; the second made the merger stick—for, as history reminds us, it was not a foregone conclusion. Those in the first wave of Unitarian Universalist ministers had previously been either Unitarian or Universalist, and many continued to be identified as such. Outnumbered by Unitarians nearly five to one, many Universalists feared being assimilated and forgotten in the vast differences of theology, class, and tradition. The second generation of Unitarian Universalist ministers still held memories and experiences of pre-merger Unitarian Universalism. They are the ones who went to work to make that which we have created viable, recognizable, and strong. Both of these "generations" still dominate our ministerial ranks and leadership.

Now comes a third wave of our ministry. While the first and second waves of Unitarian Universalist ministers are members of the Silent and Baby Boom generations, the third wave is the first to include Generation-Xers, born roughly between 1961 and 1980, as a significant presence. With Gen-Xers having been written off by sociologists as a generation hopelessly damaged by too much television, consumerism, and broken families, among other breakdowns in the social fabric (thus the moniker "X"), now is the moment in cultural history to take note of what has actually taken place. We Generation Xers have not allowed ourselves to be dismissed so easily, and now we're taking up positions in leadership and professional life. And we tend to do things differently, our mentors and elders tell us.

This third wave of ministers is made up of those who have experienced only post-merger Unitarian Universalism. As the essays in this book describe us, we often serve as a bridge by the very nature of our placement on the Unitarian Universalist historical timeline. Unitarian Universalism, born in 1961 (incidentally, the same year that postmodernism was recognized as a trend), in many ways parallels much of the Generation X struggle. The questions that these Generation X ministers ask of the movement are, in many ways, indicative of how the movement is reflecting upon itself; for we are the leaders produced by such a faith.

As we gathered the authors for this collection, we asked one primary driving question: What do you want to say to the movement at this time in your ministry? In gathering the voices for submission, we made a serious effort to pay attention to our own inclusion and exclusion of diversity. Let this anthology be a beginning, a slice of a whole that we know is larger, and a catalyst for conversation and change. Continued opportunities offer themselves for reflection on these essays, to give voice to ideas not captured here, and to begin the conversation on our website at www.rev-x.net.

x x x

What will happen as Generation X takes its place in leadership? What you will find in the pages that follow are the voices of Generation X ministers claiming their religious identity in this world, speaking back to a movement that has shaped them. They are voices that ache to articulate what is missing. **Josh Pawelek** asks us to claim the angst of the dead rock stars who inform our understanding of the world. **Krista Taves** yearns for our churches to offer an *experience* of the Ultimate. **Nancy McDonald Ladd** calls us to question the purpose of the sanctuary and the church. **Jennifer Crow** wants to know if we are intentionally holding ourselves back from becoming relevant in this world. **John Cullinan** points us to the idol worship of the First Principle. **Marlin Lavanhar** takes on the use and misuse of the Principles and Purposes. **Bret Lortie** asks whether we may be forgetting spiritual practice. **David Pyle** speaks to the struggles of being a UU military chaplain living out his faith in a troubled world. **Tamara Lebak** asks whether the sacred cow of "Joys and Concerns" in fact promotes church dysfunction. **Shana Lynngood** suggests that we have belittled the power of our message. **Erik David Carlson** urges us to stake our claim on the World Wide Web. **Joseph Santos-Lyons** warns us that white privilege still permeates UU culture. **Michael Tino** questions our commitment to youth and young-adult ministry.

X X X

As the editors discussed the creation of this collection, a vision of the possible became clear. Does every batch of new ministers who emerge from academic training believe that they have something new to say to the movement? Does the process of ministerial formation simply churn out optimism that becomes but a faded memory after the reality of "doing ministry" hits? We are likely echoing the optimism of our forbears, framed in the context of a new era. In documenting the voices of this generation of ministers at this point in their ministries, we have, at the very least, set a benchmark to use as time passes. As for any significant impact these essays may have on Unitarian Universalism, only time will tell.

TAMARA LEBAK AND BRET LORTIE
April 2008

DEAD ROCK STARS, GLOBAL INSECURITY, AND THE SPIRITUAL LIFE OF GENERATION X

Joshua Mason Pawelek

I walk deeper and deeper into the rushing water. . . . The water enters my belly button and it freezes my chest, my arms, my neck. It reaches my mouth, my nose, my ears and the roar is loud—this roar, this clapping of hands. . . .

I submerge myself in the pool completely. I grab my knees and I forget gravity and I float, and yet, even here, I hear the roar of water, the roar of clapping hands.

These hands—the hands that care, the hands that mold; the hands that touch the lips, the lips that speak the words—the words that tell us we are whole.

—Douglas Coupland,
Life After God

I bring many assumptions to the writing of this essay. At least two are in direct conflict with each other. First, the notion that the label "Generation X" somehow accurately describes the members of the United States population born between 1960 and 1980 (or whatever the dates may be) is silly. Any attempt to characterize a whole generation using cool-sounding phrases and sweeping generalizations will ultimately fail. Second, the members of the U.S. population born between 1960 and 1980 do share a common historical experience that gives them a unique and compelling spiritual worldview. Although there are not as

1

many Gen-Xers as "Baby Boomers" in the U.S. population, congregations that envision themselves thriving two to three decades from now would be wise not only to pay attention to this spiritual worldview but also to begin encouraging, developing, and—dare I say it?—*following* the leadership of those who profess it.

I also bring many lenses to the writing of this essay. On my better days I view the world through the clear lens of a theistic Unitarian Universalist, accountable, anti-racist, feminist, queer ally, liberal, and suburban American pastor dedicated to transformative preaching, teaching, healing, and social-justice struggle. I am fearless, engaged, full of conviction, and connected to a variety of justice-seeking communities. On my less-than-better days I view the world through the slightly hazy lens of a middle-class citizen of the United States, a lifelong New Englander, aware of my many privileged identities (white, male, heterosexual, able-bodied), grateful for many blessings (a great marriage, children, steady work, strong family ties, good health), but still somehow anxious about my own future and, therefore, focused on what I need to do secure that future. On my not-so-good days I view the world through the near-opaque lens of one who is juggling too many tasks and not doing any of them well; not spending enough time with my wife or kids; stressed out, moody, a little guilty; and not grounded in my "better days" mission that I described at the beginning of this paragraph. On all my days, I am a member of Generation X. I have been serving as a Unitarian Universalist parish minister since 1999, and I believe I know something about what Gen-Xers bring to ministry in these early years of the 21st century.

By 2008 the term "Generation X" has become little more than an outdated demographic label with a specific social image—the "slacker"—that was embraced and promoted by the advertising industry in the early 1990s for its effectiveness in selling cars, clothing, movies, music, and other merchandise to young adults and youth. As a generational marker, it refers loosely to people born between 1960 and 1980 in the United States (although the term—and the stereotype—have had traction in other first-world nations). Demographers often differ on what the defining dates should be, but never by more than a few years. The term began appearing in United States popular culture around the time the hip Canadian writer Douglas Coupland published his novel *Generation X* in 1991. Before Coupland, "Generation X" was the name of a late 1970s British punk-rock band fronted by singer Billy Idol. The idea for the band's name came from yet another book. Idol's mother had owned a copy of *Generation X*, published in 1964 by Jane Deverson and Charles Hamblett—a popular (not to mention shocking) sociological study of countercultural British teenagers. Drug use, premarital and casual sex, unconventional and flamboyant clothing, rejection of authority—especially parental—and alienation from religion were the defining characteristics of Deverson and Hamblett's Generation X.

In the 1990s we heard that Gen-Xers were the first fully computer-literate generation; the first generation in American history to earn a lower income overall in terms of real dollars than their parents; the first generation to enter adulthood with the expectation that middle-class women would work outside the home, earning a wage; the first generation to enter adulthood after the civil rights movement; and the only generation so far to grow up during a war in which the United States clearly lost. Furthermore, we heard in the 1990s that this generation was angry, angst-ridden, apprehensive about the future, pessimistic, cynical, politically apathetic, and, therefore, inconsequential as a voting block, socially uninterested and uninteresting. I'm reminded that in France it came to be known as *Génération Bof*—meaning, essentially, "Generation Whatever." In some ways the Generation X label was and is arbitrary, a manufactured identity. And in some ways it pointed—and still points—to a real set of experiences that cultivate a real identity. But the line is blurry. I'm never entirely sure which is which. One of the most dangerous things we do is attach labels to groups of people to explain their behavior or worldview. No label we devise can ever account for the full humanity of another person or group of people. And no group of people, no matter how similar, is monolithic. And thus, as we talk about Generation X, or any social group, we ought to acknowledge that while we may be speaking the truth, we may also be making it up—or a little of both.

I am fairly certain that the standard Generation X image in television, movies and advertising in the 1990s described an exceedingly limited subset of the generation: white, middle-and upper-class, college-educated people. Maybe that's why it appealed to me. Every time *Newsweek* or *Time* or the *Boston Globe* or the *Boston Phoenix* (I spent the 1990s in Boston) published an article on Generation X (as if there were actually something newsworthy about an advertising gimmick), we could always expect a photo of a handsome, multiracial group of young adults on the front cover. But the article itself was always about a white, middle-class, educated experience. The slacker image is a case in point. As far as I could tell in the 1990s, and as far as I can tell today, a slacker is someone who has enough money and time that he or she can afford to appear lazy and disheveled and work part-time in a record store, bookstore, coffee shop, or convenience store. A woman I dated in the very early '90s was as disheveled and grungy as they come—on the street, people thought she was poor—but she also had a $500,000 trust fund and drove a fancy sports car. Similarly, after spending four years at an elite liberal-arts college, I had moved to Boston to play rock music. My lifestyle was fairly Bohemian—an apartment in Allston shared with other rock musicians; a rehearsal space in the basement; a near-poverty-line income derived from work secured through temp agencies; a fascination with grunge music and the grunge image; a lot of time spent hanging out in rock clubs; and the security of upper-middle-class parents who supported me in my musical aspirations and were always willing to give me extra money when I needed it. I don't know that I ever crossed the line into true "slackerhood," but I came close. I doubt that I could have successfully lived this way for more than three months had I not been white, middle-class, and college-educated. I had sufficient racial and class privilege not to need a real job—but I could have gotten one had I needed one.

Real working-class people didn't—and don't—slack. Working-class people, now as then, cannot afford to slack because of the crushing economic realities of being poor in the United States. On the contrary, working-class people often work at more than one full-time job just to survive economically. No slacking there. People of color cannot afford to appear lazy and unkempt on purpose, because the realities of institutional racism require them to present an impeccable, professional image in the workplace. Most of the young black and Latino people I knew in those years (either in work settings or educational settings) had too much pride and confidence to dress poorly and behave with the cynical, jaded, "whatever" air associated with Generation X. The images attached to Generation X are, at best, limiting and exclusive and, at worst, just plain wrong.

And yet there has also always been something about the Generation X image that rings true for me, something about the personal and social challenges we Gen-Xers face today—challenges that I believe are ultimately spiritual. There are many ways to discern the truth behind the image. The path I'd like to follow in this essay is that of dead rock stars.

I was born in the spring of 1967. Soon after my birth Jimi Hendrix performed in front of 200,000 people at the Monterey Pop Festival in California, launching a stellar though short-lived career. In summer 1969, when I was two years old, Hendrix performed "The Star-Spangled Banner" at

Woodstock, in part his way of critiquing the Vietnam War. Two years later he was dead from a drug overdose. Looking at Hendrix's career, and looking at the 1960s in general, I note two streams of idealism operating among the Baby Boomers as they entered adulthood in the 1960s. First, some of those revered by the Boomers—people like Martin Luther King, Jr., Malcolm X, and Bobby Kennedy (as well as Unitarian Universalists like the Rev. James Reeb and Viola Liuzzo)—were killed for acting on behalf of their political and spiritual convictions. That was one side of the social upheaval of the 1960s. Without wanting to belittle whatever social and political concern Jimi Hendrix had for black civil rights, ending the war in Vietnam, and ending the war on poor people in the United States, let me suggest that the other idealism of the 1960s is represented by Hendrix's death from a drug overdose in September 1970. His immortal words "'Scuse me, while I kiss the sky," from the song "Purple Haze," point to the other side of the 1960s generational mindset, the notion of a counterculture marked by widespread drug use, casual sex or "free love," and experimental, communal, antiauthoritarian and sometimes hedonistic lifestyles. (I note obvious parallels with the original Generation X as described in Deverson and Hamblett's 1964 study of British teenagers. I also note that though this counterculture idealism is often what we remember about the 1960s, it also does not characterize the entire young-adult culture of the 1960s.) In the counterculture people understood themselves to be pushing their humanity to its limits, experiencing feelings, emotions, visions, and ways of being that went far beyond the conventions of the previous generation. Pushing the limits often entailed risk, and when the pushing included abusing drugs and alcohol, accidental death always loomed as a possibility. Jimi Hendrix, Janis Joplin, Jim Morrison, Gram Parsons—we might even include Elvis in this list—died, in the midst of great success, from overdoses.

Jerry Garcia died more recently from the long-term effects of drug use. Others like Mick Jagger, Keith Richards, and Eric Clapton could easily have died in the throes of drug addiction, but through fairly heroic efforts and years of hard work, each was able to kick the habit.

A lot has changed during the lifetime of Generation X. The idealism of the 1960s dissipated as the 1970s progressed; it had all but vanished as a national trait by the 1980s. I find it ironic that when the first Bush administration invaded Panama in December 1989 and United States soldiers surrounded the presidential palace in Panama City waiting to catch Manuel Noriega, the troops blasted rock music in the palace courtyard for three days. I remember hearing that music during a live newscast, and what song was playing? Jimi Hendrix's "Purple Haze." "'Scuse me, while I kiss the sky." Hendrix, who had spoken against the Vietnam War from the concert stage, was now being deployed as a psychological weapon in an incestuous little war in Central America, searching for the ex–CIA operative turned international drug king in charge of Panama. Yes, by the end of the 1980s, as Generation X was entering adulthood, things were different.

Of course Generation X has its share of rock stars who died from drug overdoses (Lane Staley of the band Alice in Chains—heroin, most likely— and Shannon Hoon of the band Blind Melon—cocaine). But controversial rap artist Eric Lynn Wright, known as Eazy-E, died of AIDS in 1995. So much for free love! When it comes to sexual behavior, AIDS has changed everything. The price of unsafe sex can be death.

Rappers Biggie Smalls and Tupac Shakur were murdered not for their positions on national politics or civil rights, but as a result of infighting in the hip-hop community, an East Coast–West Coast phenomenon that I don't hear much about anymore and never pretended to understand when it was happening in the 1990s. It always looked like gang warfare, though I couldn't tell if actual gangs were involved. Either way, so much for peace, love, and understanding! As in so many United States inner cities, disputes that used to be settled with fists, and maybe sticks or knives, are now settled with guns and typically result in death.

Finally, consider Kurt Cobain, the damaged, principled, working-class, grunge anti-hero, the leader of the seminal 1990s rock band Nirvana, who took heroin not to experiment, not to alter his mind in the fashion of his 1960s predecessors, but to escape the physical pain of his depression. Cobain wrote the song that launched the grunge revolution, "Smells Like Teen Spirit." In this song Cobain sarcastically (in my opinion) screams his now-immortal words about young people in our impulse-driven, quick-fix society, "Here we are now, entertain us." He concludes in his haunting, broken voice, warning us like a biblical prophet to beware "a denial, a denial, a denial, a denial," over and over again. Denial. That, I believe, is how Cobain understood his generation.

I'm not entirely sure why Kurt Cobain took his own life. It had something to do with personal pain and, in an odd way, with his principles, with his notion of living an authentic life, which at some level he felt he wasn't able to do. He didn't want to be a rock star. He wanted to be human, he wanted to be whole; and he lost hope that that could ever be possible for him. Those who knew him might see it differently, but that is how I see it—and I've never heard anyone say otherwise.

Kurt Cobain's experience is not typical of Generation X. But at the same time, he represents a possibility. It is extreme, but a possibility nevertheless, and thus his death haunts us. He hit rock bottom physically, emotionally, and mentally. Some might say he was always there. We too can hit rock bottom. We can come to a point in our lives when nothing seems to make sense anymore, when the pain is so great that we feel like giving up. It may be the underlying truth of Generation X that, for most of us, in the back of our minds there's a little voice, a hunch that says: life is not entirely secure—not in the way we were taught it would be.

In 2008, as the older Gen-Xers begin entering middle age, many global issues inform us of our relative insecurity: terrorism and war, violent religious fundamentalism, climate change and global warming, increasing energy demand with serious questions about how that demand is to be met, pandemics both real (AIDS) and predicted (avian flu), and a whole range of intractable economic problems within the United States and globally as the financial elite grow wealthier and the average person finds it harder and harder to make ends meet. Maybe this is nothing new. Every generation has its sources of insecurity. Baby Boomers remember training for nuclear attacks by hiding under classroom desks in the 1950s. But I don't think I'm wrong to suggest that, especially with all the evidence supporting the reality of global climate change and the potential environmental catastrophes we and our children are likely to face, and especially in the wake of the September 11, 2001, terrorist attacks on the World Trade Center in New York City and the Pentagon in Washington, D.C., the sense of insecurity is large and growing. Each of us figures out the truth of our insecurity in our own way, and when we do, it can be terrifying. The question I want readers and congregations to ponder is this: When you finally come face to face with the terrible realization that life is going to be less secure than you expected, what do you do so as not to give up? How do you respond? Or, if you've already been there, how did you survive? How do you find hope when you possess increasingly reliable evidence that the future is not as bright as you once dreamed?

Pay attention to your answer to this question, because in it you will discover that which is most holy in your life—that which matters most dearly; that which makes your life worth living. For me, finding that answer is the heart of Generation X spirituality. In the end, Kurt Cobain didn't have an answer—at least not one he could use to save himself. There was a rupture between him and the sacredness of life, a gulf too big for him to bridge.

Well, it's time for bridging, and I see Unitarian Universalist congregations as great locations for such bridging. But let us be careful in how we proceed. Most of the "church-studies" literature I've encountered about how to appeal to Generation X (as well as to Baby Boomers) is not helpful, and may in fact be harmful. Most of that literature, at some point, suggests that *spiritual seeking* is the dominant trait of both Generation X and the Baby Boomers. People of both generations have been socialized as consumers; they don't necessarily have strong allegiances to the religion of their childhood; and they are looking for high value in a local congregation. Denominational affiliation is not as important as finding the right fit. Correct theology and doctrine are not as important (at least among liberal religious types) as finding exciting, visionary ministry. Adherence to tradition is not as important as finding a vibrant, multigenerational community. Gen-Xers and Baby Boomers alike, the literature tells us, are looking for dynamic, provocative preaching, uplifting and participatory music, excellent religious education for children, and a visible presence in the community with respect to social justice issues.

Blah, blah, blah! Who isn't looking for these things? Of course these are all important components of successful congregations. But my experience of the church-studies literature on generational needs and expectations is that it has yet to identify Generation X (and often fails even to identify Baby Boomers) as congregational leaders. Consumers, yes, but leaders, no. Seekers, yes, but not people with their own vision for how the congregation ought to be. The literature makes lofty (though often too abstract) statements about what people are looking for—and about the fact that they are looking in earnest—but it doesn't see them as responsible for the life of the church. It reduces a whole generation to the identity of savvy spiritual shoppers. Ironically, although it implies that these shoppers view the local church as a commodity, the literature also trains the local church to relate to these shoppers as commodities. They become the people to whom we, as pastors and congregational leaders, must appeal if we want to grow in the 21st century. They add value to our religious community. Thus, we want to attract them. What are the spiritual "impulse items" we can put on display to get them to come back a second time? Everyone and everything becomes a commodity, and spirit wanes. Kurt Cobain sang about denial. I wonder if, in following the advice of the church-studies literature, we are sinking into deep denial about our common humanity, about authentic spirituality, and about the power of both to respond to the growing insecurity in our world. Mutual commodification is not a spiritual path. I suspect that it was this same dynamic in the context of the music industry—commodification of music and the artists who create and perform it, combined with a corresponding and insidious commodification of the fans who consume it— that exacerbated Kurt Cobain's depression to the point that he committed suicide.

No more commodification! Of course people are shopping and seeking. That's what happens in a religiously pluralistic society. It is no great insight to say that people are shopping and seeking. If they weren't shopping or seeking, they wouldn't visit our congregations. Of course we want them to return next week, and there are things we can do to inspire them to do so. But what I really care about as a pastor is not the best practices for appealing to a generation of people who may or may not fit a certain stereotype, but the reality of insecurity in the lives of those who attend worship, whether they are longtime members or visiting for the first time. As a worship leader, a religious educator, a pastoral caregiver and a social-justice leader, can I demonstrate that I know about and experience insecurity? Can I demonstrate that I know why it exists and how it shapes people's lives for the worse— that it can lead, if unchecked, to self-destruction and social decay? Can I demonstrate that the God to whom I bow my head in prayer responds to me in the midst of my insecurity and justifies in me an attitude of hopefulness and love? And can I demonstrate, in response to God, a way of being in the world that counters the forces of oppression, violence, and greed that breed insecurity? If I can do all this and it doesn't lead to numerical growth, then so be it. But I refuse to conduct a ministry that seeks to appeal to some abstract spiritual shopper at the expense of dealing with real issues, truth-telling, fighting oppression and—dare I say it?—professing a saving message that overcomes insecurity, fear, and selfishness. No more commodification!

Insecurity is a real force in the lives of Generation X as well as in the lives of those generations coming after us. And let's be honest—insecurity is an increasingly real force in the lives of those who are older than us. One of the more popular ways to deal with insecurity in the United States these days, for young and old alike, is to seek out an apocalyptic religion that interprets all sources of insecurity as signs of the End Time. Such religions tend to prescribe strict behavioral codes and to demand adherence to these codes as the price for salvation once the world ends. While I appreciate the sense of security such religions instill—on some level I envy it!—my concern is that they never actually seek to transform the social, political, economic, and environmental problems that cause insecurity in the first place. They wall themselves off inside righteous enclaves, awaiting the end (which never comes), not caring what happens in the larger world. For me, this behavior suggests extreme denial. For Unitarian Universalists, for liberal religious people, this kind of apocalypticism isn't generally appealing as a way to address the sources of insecurity. If I may be so bold, let me suggest a broad spiritual pattern I discern among liberal religious people—and particularly among Gen-Xers—as we attempt to deal with insecurity.

First, we develop a sense that something is wrong with the world. We notice a subtle, sometimes dull, sometimes acute nagging around the edges of our consciousness, a tugging at our heartstrings. Something is not right with the world: racism, homophobia, wars for oil, economic imperialism, global warming, etc. "I move deeper and deeper into the rushing water."[1]

Second, after sensing that something is wrong with the world, we become mired in cynicism. This is our trap, our false security. Cynicism is appealing because it allows us to place blame in the laps of others. It's a way of relieving a personal sense of responsibility. Cynicism is comfortable, it's familiar, and all our friends are doing it. Sometimes cynicism is so paralyzing that we don't even recognize we are lying prone on the floor. In the end cynicism is no more effective at transforming the world than the mindset of the Christian fundamentalist who is simply waiting for the end of the world. The net result is the same: nothing changes. "The water enters my belly button and it freezes my chest, my arms, my neck. It reaches my mouth, my nose, my ears and the roar is loud—this roar, this clapping of hands."

Third—and this is where congregations can make a huge difference; indeed, this is where congregations are essential; this is where congregations can be of most service to Generation X and all those who are insecure in these times—we admit that beneath our cynicism is a sense of insecurity, along with sadness, anger, fear, and other difficult emotions. Congregations can be locations where one is safe and even encouraged to admit insecurity—not an easy thing for Unitarian Universalists and other liberal religious people to do. "I submerge myself in the water completely."

Fourth, we begin to engage in theological reflection. If I am truly a person of faith, then what is the content of my faith, and how does it respond to what is wrong in the world and how I feel about it? If I am to have an authentic spiritual life, then what is the content of that spiritual life, and how does it respond to what is wrong in the world and how I feel about it? What is sacred to me? What is holy to me? What matters most to me? How does all of it respond to what is wrong in the world and how I feel about it? "I grab my knees and I forget gravity and I float, and yet, even here, I hear the roar of water, the roar of clapping hands."

Finally, we take responsibility. We make ourselves accountable. As people of faith we enter into a variety of saving struggles. We address our insecurities—and the insecurities of the world—by constructing lives that counter the very sources of that insecurity. We don't wait for the end of the world. We work for the survival of the world now. This is Generation X at its best. This is the new counterculture—not ultimately overwhelmed by insecurity, but motivated, hopeful, dedicated, and ready to lead in the church and society. "These hands—the hands that care, the hands that mold; the hands that touch the lips, the lips that speak the words—the words that tell us we are whole."

NOTE

1. Coupland, Douglas, *Life After God* (New York: Pocket Books, 1994), p. 360.

UNITARIAN UNIVERSALISM AND THE HUNGER FOR RELIGIOUS IDENTITY

NANCY MCDONALD LADD

I. FOR THE LOVE OF CHURCH

I love church. I've always loved church. I love the humming noise that rises from the church kitchen, the familiar clank and gurgle of activity welcoming me with open arms and fresh coffee each Sunday morning, the eager rows of hymnals awaiting the arrival of their attendant singers, the bevy of children running wild through the fellowship hall dodging the knees and ankles of a whole village of adults who couldn't imagine life without them. I love the fourth-grade boy who stands on tiptoes to pull my ears every time he sees me and the quiet care of the member who makes sure the fridge is stocked with caffeine-rich Coca-Cola to keep the minister awake and characteristically perky at early meetings.

I love church so much—church itself, that act of being together in a, shall we say, "churchy" way—that each day when I arrive for work at the congregation I serve, I make a point of entering the building through the tall arching doors of the sanctuary. Rather than beginning my day by walking through the conveniently located door near the church office, I set the tone of the morning by walking down the wood-floored aisle, past the candle stubs lit for our joys and sorrows, and alongside the pulpit, where I try to find something to say that's worth breaking the silence for every Sunday morning. Only then, once I've gotten my fill of our sacred space, do I move on toward the office where other needs await.

When I am tired or doubtful, which is more often than I like to admit, I sometimes pause halfway up the aisle, choose a pew somewhere toward the middle and take a few moments for prayer to remind myself what I loved about this work in the first place and what I love about it still.

I love church. I don't love e-mail. I don't love copy machines and phone calls and busy schedules. I don't even love potluck parties and coffee-talk and committee meetings. *I love church.* I do those other things because they make *church*, in all of its evocative, heart-healing and tragically flawed glory, available for me and for the people I am called to serve.

My love for church, for that numinous something that I've found only in religious community, is the reason for my ministry. It's patched me together when I couldn't do the patching by myself. It's lifted me up into the fellowship of trusted friends when I needed it most. It's challenged me to ask more of myself and others than I ever could have without it. My love for the institution of church, that love that lies at the core of my call to the ministry, leads me to be alternately bemused, frustrated, and deeply saddened when I hear my fellow Unitarian Universalists say things like, "I'm not really that religious. I'm a Unitarian Universalist." In those moments spent fielding worries that our congregational life is "too churchy" for some or "too religious" for others, I struggle to remain responsive and pastorally effective.

As a minister, I hear these things from people I respect and honor. I'm not so pompous as to imagine that such statements are "wrong" in any unqualified way. I know very well that the common Unitarian Universalist desire to distance ourselves from all things too glaringly formal or stereotypically churchlike is grounded in reason and, occasionally, even in deeply held theology. I know that the freedom to abandon traditional forms and to move toward a more widely embracing and amorphous concept of Unitarian Universalist identity is precisely what brought many current members of our congregations to our faith.

But I also know that this desire to distance ourselves from the religiosity that lies at the core of our identity has a great deal to do with a tragic lack of imagination, an inability to define religion as anything other than a tightly binding stereotype of authority and dominance, and an unwillingness to see religion as anything more than a stereotype worth running away from. Our fear of being religious has a great deal to do with our avoidance of important questions about what it means for a free-thinker to be proudly, powerfully, and boldly religious.

Instead of grappling with our religious tradition, we too often turn our backs on it and redefine the ties that bind us together in purely secular terms. Rather than seeking to deepen our relationship to it, we have too often chosen to ignore it and to select for ourselves an entirely new, often blatantly anti-religious self identity.

This proud and hard-fought distance between ourselves and traditional "religion" is not a part of my own story. It is someone else's story, but it is not mine. After all, I love church, and as the highest expression of my love for church, I most certainly have a deep and abiding love for religion and its expression in the act of communal worship.

I am incapable of showing up on Sunday morning for the weekly gathering of a Unitarian Universalist community to give a secularized message with an eye toward teaching everyone something. All I know how to do is show up on Sunday morning for the weekly worship of a congregation of faith dedicated to the deepening of spiritual lives and the sharpening of moral sensibilities.

To that end, I am careful as a preacher to limit the number of sermons I preach that exist mostly to persuade listeners to have a specific opinion about a social or political issue. When I do preach such topical sermons, I try to do so with the intention of moving each listener toward a deep spiritual engagement with the issue. Rather than persuading a person to be a vegetarian or to drive a hybrid car or to vote against a certain piece of legislation, worship and preaching should engage the worshiper in a process of discerning what actions they are called to through the living out of their own theological and religious values.

Thus, worship, to me, is an inherently different thing from a community forum or an educational opportunity, two worthwhile but distinctly non-religious activities that our Unitarian Universalist worship services too often resemble.

It's simply not possible for me to present our time together on Sunday morning as anything but a worshipful enterprise, grounded in an intentionally religious set of liturgical practices and a particular religious worldview that arises from our rich theological heritage as Unitarian Universalists. *This religious worldview encompasses an idea of the divine as that which is worthy of reverence and the church as a place that we turn to for more than just political persuasion, affirmation of our existing beliefs, and a sense of community. I think our religious heritage calls us to see the church as a place for personal and social transformation in relation to the sacred, and that religious heritage is not something that I want to escape. I have experienced truly transformative and spiritually challenging worship in my life, and I believe that such worship is a more effective tool for changing the world than any partisan diatribe posing as worship could ever be.*

Standing with my family around my grandmother's coffin with the ancient liturgies of the Roman Catholic funeral mass sounding in the air around us, I found that the act of worship helped me to let go of any resentment I might have held. I heard that God loved her, as God loves us all, and I left that moment utterly changed. Listening to my own minister in the first UU church I ever attended preach about being more concerned with the salvation of this world than salvation in the next, I left that sanctuary knowing that theologically grounded social action was a part of the religious journey. And, most recently, when the people of the congregation I serve raised our hands in silent support of every committed relationship, gay and straight, the members of my own church knew what it must feel like to have a truly open table of communion, informed by our faith, from which no hungry person is turned away.

On Sunday morning, all I know how to do is worship. It is what I have to offer. Not entertainment. Not technological wizardry. Not a forum for prolonged scientific or literary debate. Worship. Worship that evokes a shared story. Worship that takes us out of our own individual struggles to succeed and into a communal effort to make the world into a place more consistent with liberal religious values, a world with less resentment, more thoughtful action, and more truly open tables.

That's what I hope for, though some days are always more hopeful than others. I long for worship, and I long to be able to create it in meaningful and evocative ways within our unique religious tradition.

The word "worship" may or may not imply an active and present deity that one may choose to call God. Worship absolutely does, however, involve a connection to something inclusive of, but larger than, our individual selves. Maybe that something is God. Maybe it isn't. Maybe it is the very unlikely presence of hope in the middle of all our muddling through. I've come to find that the name we choose for the object of our worship, if we choose to name it at all, matters remarkably little to me. What matters is the intentionality with which we meet each Sunday morning.

My intention each Sunday morning is to connect to the source of our hope and challenge, the object of our reverence, and the reason for our actions in the world. This, sadly, is not often enough the intention of shared Unitarian Universalist worship.

Too often, we gather simply to be a place where liberal folks can get together, an intentionally separate intellectual and political elite, united so as to set ourselves apart from the surrounding community rather than to be of service to it. Too often, we gather to be around people and ideas that we perceive to be "like us" rather than around people and ideas that challenge us to grow and change. Too often, we gather just for the sake of our own limited sense of community, and from my perspective, this just isn't enough.

If we gather with the intention simply of creating community in the midst of isolation, community is likely all that we will find. If we gather to profess an intentionally exclusive partisan or liberal worldview, that world-view will be the end result of our efforts. But if we gather to worship and to ask the humble question of how we might serve, we may find the depth that really transforms.

Worship is, as James Luther Adams says, "where the intimate and the ultimate meet." It is where our hurts and hopes and those of the world come together. Meeting with that kind of deep intentionality, that kind of reverent hope, changes lives—just as my own life has been changed by the worship experiences that shape my ministry.

In his advice to new ministers, I once heard a distinguished colleague remind us that what we do in worship is deeply religious work. When you enter the church, he said, "Take off your shoes, for you are standing on holy ground." Remember that the ground beneath our feet, no matter what the terrain, is sanctified by the act of worship. Remember that you stand on holy ground. Every Sunday, even when ministering to those for whom the concept of "religion" itself is troubling, I try not to forget his words.

I struggle greatly with that impulse in our denomination to identify congregations as containers for community and like-mindedness, and I do so not just as a minister, but as a young adult, one born in the 1970s whose parents' generation responded to the cultural and religious pressures of their age by breaking down the idols of the generations before them.

In our own movement, many leaders of the past 40 years have, in their own ways, challenged the embryonic entity of post-merger Unitarian Universalism to live into the challenge of our heretical forebears. If part of our contemporary challenge is to understand and come to know the unique heritage of our faith, it cannot be denied that the often-rich religious humanism that came to the fore in the past 40 years brought with it creativity and vision that have served our congregations well.

Following the example and guidance of clergy like the Rev. Kenneth Patton, the leaders of the last decades brought dance to the sanctuary and creativity to the pulpit. They pushed open a window to Eastern theologies once explored by the transcendentalists and enlivened the intellectual humanism of the 1930s and 1940s with a new, sometimes deeply reverent, religious naturalism that has nurtured many young clergy, including me.

Now we are the inheritors of this Baby-Boom revolution in liberal religious practice. Now we're here, and in an utterly unsurprising turn of events, it's our turn to rebel. How does a new generation of Unitarian Universalist religious leaders rebel against the generations of iconoclasts who preceded them? I find that some of us are rebelling by reaching back into our ecclesiastical history to find traces of what it must have been like to be an overtly religious community of liberal faith.

While I cannot speak for all, perhaps not even most, of the young adults in our movement, I can say that a significant proportion of the young adults in my congregation and a number of my young colleagues find ourselves settling down comfortably into the churchy pews that seemed to rankle the rebellious backsides of our parents even as we open the hymnal to sing "Amazing Grace" with throaty reverence. Some of us even talk about how much we like Jesus, even if most of us don't think he's God, and we gird ourselves with stoles and robes and stories of the generations before our parents and our parents' parents. We respond to the skepticism about religion present in the previous decades by seeking out ways to be lovingly, proudly, and actively religious now.

While I have characterized this move toward a more traditional religious understanding of church as an aspect of one generation's rebellious response to its predecessors, I must admit that such a claim is only partially true. In reality, the trends that shape the theological and practical identity of Unitarian Universalism have never divided along purely generational boundaries. Across the board, from youth and young adults to clergy in the twilight of their careers, people within our movement who are hungry for meaning are looking toward our religious heritage as a way to ground our movement in a particular way of being and doing church as we move confidently into our future. As the following pages will show, even a cursory survey of contemporary American ecumenical thought illustrates that we are not alone in our search for a distinct and theologically grounded religious identity for our faith.

II. THE LOSS OF IDENTITY

Part of my continuing-education work includes participating in an ecumenical program called the First Parish Project. Sponsored by a grant from the Eli Lilly Foundation, the project brings together young-adult clergy from all over the country and from many denominations. Over the course of two years, we meet every few months at a rural North Carolina retreat center to discuss all sorts of things pertinent to effective and responsible ministry. During those meetings, we have focused on issues like evangelism, pastoral care, and the pastor's spiritual life. However, as is often the case, the most important learning happens outside the formal program. The good stuff happens during the chilly evening conversations we share while sitting in rocking chairs on the bunkhouse porch. In those wee hours, we talk about how we can be authentic servants to our congregations and authentic practitioners of our faith traditions.

Most of my colleagues in this group are from the mainline Protestant traditions, with Lutherans and Methodists especially well represented. Some of our theologies differ in profound and marked ways. In many cases, our traditions teach us very different things about God and Jesus, and yet our personal similarities, and the forces at work within our traditions, seem far more striking to all of us than our differences.

Almost to a person, my young-adult colleagues find themselves responding to what they see as the loss of denominational identity over the last few decades. A Methodist friend decries the loss of a clear Methodist theology among some in his denomination. Watered-down Methodism, polished to be more palatable, generalized, and more widely appealing, has lost its savor for him, and he searches for a way to incorporate historically grounded Methodist theology into the work of his congregation and his denomination. Another friend, from the Evangelical Lutheran Church in America, mourns the fact that some mainline churches bent on growth try to model themselves after nondenominational evangelical megachurches, losing their abiding Christian identity underneath a consumer-driven agenda and high production values.

In his book *The Transformation of American Religion*, sociologist Alan Wolfe also notices what my friends and I experience in our congregations. He identifies this loss of denominational identity as a widespread convergence of American religious practice, resulting in even markedly liberal denominations worshiping in an evangelical style.

As all of the religions in the United States begin to resemble each other in practice, they do so by resembling most those of the evangelicals. For a religious sensibility that emerged among the dispossessed, evangelical patterns of worship—joyful, emotional, personal, and emphatic on the one hand, impatient with liturgy and theologically broad to the point of incoherence on the other—has increasingly become the dominant worship style in the United States (36).

Thus, it is not altogether uncommon to walk away from the worship service of some Unitarian Universalist, Methodist, Lutheran, or evangelical nondenominational church without any clear idea of the theology or history that underlies the institution. The resistance to religious language and historical identity that we see in Unitarian Universalism today is by no means limited to our movement. Rather, it is a phenomenon we share with those very people we so often summarily dismiss—the nondenominational evangelicals.

As Unitarian Universalist congregations have moved away from articulated theologies and an overtly religious identity, they have aimed instead to become communities of education, personal edification, and civic responsibility. So too has the evangelical movement shied away from a historically grounded religious identity and toward its own theologically innocuous goals of self-help and personal betterment.

As different as we Unitarian Universalists like to think we are from the surrounding Christian-dominated religious culture, it is the sea in which we all swim. Our responses to the traditional structures of denominational American religion are patterned on the responses of those from whom we take great pains to distance ourselves. As Wolfe says, "We are all evangelicals now." Regardless of our place on the liberal/conservative spectrum, we share a common retreat from our distinct stories and religious heritage that robs us of our unique identities.

For many young adults within the mainline traditions, megachurches seem more like megamalls than congregations of deeply considered faith and action, and there is a significant subsection of young-adult worshipers who respond with great negativity to this commercialization and loss of identity within their congregations. Churches, both Unitarian Universalist and otherwise, whose worship and preaching are indistinguishable from one another and from generalized self-help pop psychology, are simply not enough. At least they're not enough for me, and if my young adult colleagues in the First Parish Project and I are correct, they're not enough for a growing number of faithful young adults across the Protestant spectrum.

There we sit, 13 young ministers at the First Parish Project, all of us working to clarify our own positions within specific traditions. We rise from that porch and go away from one another to tell very different stories to very different congregations. Then we come back together again every few months to share the same hunger—a hunger to connect to the distinct traditions that have so deeply nurtured us thus far. There we sit, our rocking chairs moving back and forth on that now-familiar porch, mourning what feels like the loss of identity within the traditions we love.

I don't want my friend's Methodist church to feel like a catch-all container for all forms of Christianity, and I don't want my friend's Lutheranism to be indistinguishable from a nondenominational megachurch. More than anything, I don't want my Unitarian Universalist religious home to feel like a catch-all container for all forms of religious practice, glossing over the challenges of each distinct practice with as much haste as a tourist on an overscheduled vacation. I want my church to feel distinct, unique, a part of a larger tradition all our own. That's what all my colleagues in this little group seem to want. Sitting there rocking and talking, my friends and I have learned from each other that we want churches that feel and act and live like churches—our churches, formed out of our distinct stories. We want to take our traditions seriously by grappling with them, telling and retelling their stories in new and theologically challenging ways. We want to remember where we come from so that we can forge ahead with a vision of the future that has grounding in a tradition we can call home.

III. Detraditionalization and Retraditionalization

Like my friends in the First Parish Project, acclaimed author Dorothy Butler Bass, in her book *The Practicing Congregation: Imagining a New Old Church*, speaks clearly from the mainline Protestant tradition, and not surprisingly her theology is very different from mine and that of most Unitarian Universalists. However, the overarching trends within American religions that she describes in her book are too familiar to discount.

Bass cites the 1970s and 1980s as periods of what she calls "rapid detraditionalization" in our society and specifically within mainline congregations. She says that "detraditionalization is a set of processes, variously described as 'post traditional' or 'postmodern,' whereby received traditions no longer provide meaning and authority in everyday life" (28).

Detraditionalization in the political, economic, and religious spheres, over the past several decades, was a direct response to previous generations' willingness to ascribe definitive power to the traditions and institutions that governed society. In the 1940s and 1950s, mainline congregations, including many Unitarian and Universalist congregations, were seen as the carriers of tradition, the stalwart bastions of authority and cultural establishment.

Mainline churches were the repositories of cultural authority, but the years immediately following the merger of the American Unitarian Association and the Universalist Church of America were a period of rapid change for the status and power of organized religion across the board in America and abroad. As a result of this changing status and authority, the received tradition became an object of intense scrutiny on both the sacred and the secular fronts. Critical reflection replaced faithful practice as the marker of responsible citizenship and engaged religious participation.

Bass quotes sociologist Paul Heelas, who says that "detraditionalization entails that people have acquired the opportunity to stand back from, critically reflect upon, and lose their faith in what the tradition has to offer. They have to arrive at a position where they can *have their own say*" (30).

Not unlike the rebellious generation of transcendentalists who came long before them, the Baby-Boom generation and its philosophical companions tore down the theological and cultural assumptions of their day and erected something both broader and more amorphous in their place.

According to Bass's theories of detraditionalization, today's Unitarian Universalism might be seen as a product of recent generations' courage to reflect critically on their tradition and embrace the power that came with *having their say*. This critical reflection is the sustained religious and ethical worldview of many Unitarian Universalists, and many justly feel it is the only true identity we have.

And yet here I am—inside our movement of widely detraditioned liberal religion—standing beside people of every age *who love church*. We embrace our unique religious identity as Unitarian Universalists by seeking new ways to redefine our treasure trove of religious inheritance. We bend over backward in worship and religious education to find relevance in our history and our rituals. We're the folks who take what my colleague Barbara ten Hove calls "wounded words"—words like grace, soul, sin and God—and examine them anew so that they can be reconstructed in meaningful ways from the ashes of their limiting old definitions.

We are engaged in the work of *retraditioning*. To retradition a movement whose very rebellion has given it a voice is not a process that I or anyone else should take lightly, nor is a replacement for the *detraditioning* that has become a substantial part of our identity. Rather, it is a part of the spiritual landscape of today's Unitarian Universalism, a landscape in which people of every generation find themselves surrounded on all sides by a fragmented society and come to church to have one single place in their lives where they know they're part of a story that is inclusive of and greater than themselves.

People come to church in this fragmented world not only to have their say but also to hear a story worth telling and to locate themselves somewhere within an embracing tradition of faith. People come to church to be a part of something; to have some ground to stand on while the whole world shifts beneath them. They come to hear a story that includes them but is infinitely bigger than them. They come not just to be heard, not just to have their say, but also to be embraced and to be challenged and to be called out to a particular form of renewed discipleship.

Retraditioning is not a usurpation of the detraditioning with which it interacts. Rather, according to Bass, it's a way of living out our unique identity while continuing to respond in new ways to the pressures of contemporary society:

> Retraditioning is a simpler concept than its awkward name implies. It is a process wherein individuals—and congregations—are responding to the larger cultural results of modern fragmentation by creating communities that provide sacred space for the formation of identity and meaning, the construction of "pockets" of connectedness to the long history of Christian witness and practice in a disconnected world (50).

Of course, our "pockets of connectedness" as Unitarian Universalists are not connecting us to the same long history of discipleship and witness as that of mainline Protestantism. We have our own story to tell, a story that is deeply rooted in the American Protestant tradition but is also informed by the diverse sources that have shaped liberal religion for hundreds of years.

Our particular stories are our guides, our tools for the shaping of identity. Our congregations can be retraditioned through worship and study in creative and responsive ways that take our unique religious identity seriously enough to ask what exactly it entails. Our congregations can be environments for reminding us why we are the way we are, and we can use that grounding to begin envisioning the future in the context of a challenging and theologically relevant past.

We need to teach not only UU history but also liberal theological history. We need to preach not only about the great social reformers of our movement, but also the history and heritage of the liberal religious message that guided those reformers to do what they did, a message that proclaims a deity whose primary manifestation is love and whose people are called to act out that love in their daily lives.

IV. A Case Study: The Emergent Church Goes Vintage

In the 1990s a self-described group of "post-evangelical" Christians began to have conversations about the forms of worship and Christian discipleship that could emerge from what they saw as the theology-phobic megachurches of the evangelical world. They came to call their constellation of ideas the "Emergent Church." Led by author and preacher Brian McLaren, the Emergent model has come to be synonymous with young and vibrant congregations that are firmly grounded in historic traditions and liturgies while remaining free to embrace experimentation and informality of practice. Some of these Emergent congregations are expressly attached to denominations. They subscribe to what they call a "deep ecclesiology" which insists that all particular denominational identities have unique gifts and unique shortcomings that shape the way church is lived.

One way that Emergent Church leaders describe their worship and congregational life is as contemporary Christianity with a "vintage" feel. The word vintage carries with it connotations from the ever-fickle world of fashion, where everything old is new again—like your old leg warmers from the 1980s gaining a renewed hipness if you just hang on to them long enough. As such, it feels a bit faddish to me. Yet the idea that so many youth and young adults across the country are drawn to such "vintage" Emergent churches remains compelling. While it may in fact be just another trend, it is a trend worth paying attention to.

Emergent churches tend to combine the contemporary with the traditional, interspersing time-honored Protestant prayer forms with songs by the Grateful Dead and original compositions by church members. In Emergent sanctuaries, one often sees traditional dark-varnished pews interspersed with scattered youth-lounge couches, and a central focal point of worship augmented with large video screens on which slides, lyrics, and video presentations illuminate the sanctuary along with that old familiar dappled light of stained-glass windows.

Quotes from notable Protestant theologians are stenciled on the walls alongside an abundance of visual arts. Young-adult congregants rise to speak the old words of the Apostle's Creed right before they break off into small groups for more intimate and personalized prayer experiences. The Emergent Church is a blending of the old and the new, a forum for theological discussion and a place for embodied, sometimes charismatic, worship.

One such Emergent congregation is Jacob's Well, a church that draws

1,000 worshipers, mostly young adults, to Sunday services in its traditional Presbyterian sanctuary in downtown Kansas City, Missouri. According to a September 19, 2006, article in *The Christian Century*, traditional architecture and evocative worship forms are exactly what Jacob's Well and the Emergent church movement are going for.

> If yesteryear's evangelical church was the equivalent of a starter castle in the suburbs, [Jacob's Well] is more akin to a rehabilitated loft in a gentrifying city. Whereas evangelical churches (and increasing numbers of mainline ones) seek to attract young people by designing spaces stripped of Christian symbols and tradition, JW people seem to like the traditional feel of the sanctuary, with its dark wood, stained glass and high ceilings ("A Visit to Jacob's Well: Emerging Model," by Jacob Byassee, *The Christian Century*, vol. 123, no. 19, September 19, 2006, page 20).

Much of the Emergent Church movement and its "vintage" Christianity are difficult to translate to a Unitarian Universalist context. However, the fact that thousands of young adults are flocking to refurbished inner-city sanctuaries in their dreadlocks and blue jeans to sing ancient psalms and hear about everything from the theology of Dietrich Bonhoeffer to the trials of Job does highlight the presence of a significant group of young-adult worshipers who want to grapple with distinct traditions in new ways.

Perhaps that hunger for a clear theological identity that my friends and I recognized in one another is already manifesting itself in an exodus among young adults away from amorphous non-theological post-denominational forms of worship and toward religious communities with form, scope, theological clarity, and proudly historic identities.

What would "vintage" Unitarian Universalism look like? Perhaps it would be a form of liberal religious worship that combines the innovative and the evocative, that blends the concrete and challenging theologies of our forebears with the creative and effervescent ideas of present scientific and technological advancement. "Vintage" worship might focus primarily not on "vintage" doctrine, but on a "vintage" sense of our own intentionality. Since the beginnings of American Unitarianism and Universalism and long before, our people, at their best, have gathered to worship with the intention of meeting the holy. For ages, our people have shown up on Sunday morning and have "taken off their shoes," because they knew they stood on holy ground.

At Jacob's Well, and many other congregations within the Emergent movement, young people are expressing a desire to take off their shoes before the holy and to dive into the challenges of their particular traditions. With enough trust in one another, enough confidence in the strength of our historic identity, enough love for that thing called church, might we not do the same?

V. Longing for the Living Tradition

I write these words because I too am hungry. Like all those nondenominational young-adult Christians reimagining what it means to be evangelical, I yearn for meaningful, deeply felt, intentionally practiced religion, but my chosen faith is not nondenominational Christianity. My chosen faith is Unitarian Universalism, and I, along with many others in our movement, hunger to take our tradition seriously, to leave each Sunday morning knowing I am a part of a long and ever-reaching heritage and a way of being religious that is inclusive of, but larger than, my own personal spiritual journey.

To feed that hunger, my congregation and I struggle with our "wounded words" instead of turning away from them. We dig deeply into that which makes us uncomfortable, so that from that discomfort we can open ourselves to transformation. We look with both critical and grateful eyes at our tradition, including the prevailing humanism of the last four decades, and we remember that being Unitarian Universalist means being bold, iconoclastic, devotional, and faith-filled. Sometimes all of this grappling with our tradition is difficult. Not everybody wants to examine their wounded words. It goes without saying that not everybody agrees with me. But we're trying, in at least one congregation—we're trying, like family, to be in relationship with our own people and our own heritage. In so doing, we are also trying to call to mind all the right reasons Unitarian Universalism exists as an expressly religious community.

Many of our most successful and thriving Unitarian Universalist congregations today are those places that fully embrace their identity as liberal religious communities of faith. Many of our thriving congregations are the congregations that know they exist to be and to do that mysterious thing called church.

People find their way to these congregations and to places like the Emergent Church's Jacob's Well because they offer a glimpse into a truly living tradition—not a reactionary antireligious tradition, but a living tradition that responds to its environment while continuing to tell the ever-growing story of its origins and identity.

The story I tell to new members of the congregation I serve is a story about a lineage of people who lived, died, suffered, and spoke out. I tell them stories of people like Abraham, Moses, Aaron, and Ruth, Siddhartha Gautama, Mother Teresa, and the people who fill the pages of *The Washington Post*. I even tell them stories about my very favorite iconoclast, Jesus himself. But I also tell them stories that are ours uniquely, stories about Unitarians and Universalists like Sebastian Castellio, who died for his faith; Olympia Brown, who stood up to ridicule to preach that God's love was for all people; and Lewis McGee, who wouldn't let a white denomination's discouragement stop him from doing some justice in the streets of Chicago.

I tell them these stories because these people of faith, our people of faith, did these things not simply for their secular political convictions, not simply because they liked having a community to bond with once a week, but because *their faith mattered*. Their strong religious convictions were a defining aspect of their lives. Those are our people—people who created and refined and fought for a particular way of being religious that is uniquely and spectacularly ours. Unitarian Universalism, founded on the idea that God is one and God is love, teaches us that somehow when we love one another, we connect to that which is worthy of reverence, and we make ourselves more capable of changing the world. When we take our tradition seriously, we take those religious convictions seriously, and they are quite worthy of uplifting.

If we are to continue the story our forebears began, our congregations are called to be more than locations for community activity, academic learning, and civic advancement. We are called to be *churches*, homes for the spirit, places where the mystery and the magic of religion happen within us, among us, and beyond us. We are a part of a greater story, a worldview that existed long before us, and a tradition that will continue to be elevated and developed in the generations to come.

In my work as a parish minister, I labor with the hope that our liberal religious tradition will continue to grow and thrive, to change and remember, for as long as history allows. May we live into the challenge of our forebears by having the courage to be what we have always been called to be: a richly, enthusiastically and uniquely religious community. There are many who hunger for such an expression of our shared faith. I surely count myself among them.

GOD IS IN THE FLOOR

Krista Taves

As a child I was certain that God lived in and above the old wooden floor of the sanctuary at the Oak Street United Mennonite Church in Leamington, Ontario. As I sat in my basement Sunday-school classroom learning those precious Bible stories beneath the ductwork and pipe-lined oil-paint-slathered ceiling, the adults above us in the 500-seat sanctuary did the most sacred thing of all—they worshiped. And did we ever know it! Every shift in body weight was accompanied by the creaking of that old wooden floor above our heads. When the adults stood for prayer, the wooden floor roared as 500 bodies rose in unison. When they sang, the solid resonance of 500 voices united in song pulsated through the floor so loudly that it was difficult for us to hear the teacher. And when the minister preached, we could hear his thin voice, not so clearly as to discern the words, but we knew exactly what was happening. "The Truth" was being spoken. This was my first experience of that sacred presence. I felt the power of that being in the roar of the floor, in shifting bodies and raised voices, and in the indiscernible words of the minister who preached the sacred truth to the best of his ability. As a young child not yet trained out of the magic of Santa Claus and the Risen Christ, this was awe-inspiring and comforting. God was extremely close; his—yes, at that age it was "his"—power, constancy and love jostled just overhead.

And yet, even as a young child, I knew exactly what caused the sounds. The creaks and groans and roars of God Almighty rested in the great and small shifts of human weight and in the power of the human voice. Even then, the majesty of the divine rested in the intended and unintended consequences of human choice and behavior. This made it no less powerful, no less holy, no less sacred.

From that time forward, I have expected Sunday mornings to be richly experiential. My soul aches for it. I long to be moved profoundly, and I wish to be a different person when I leave worship—different in my soul and in my body. Special. Connected. Alive. Filled with love. I yearn for the reassuring constancy of an ever-present love and the awe-inspiring inspiration of some-thing far greater than I, rooted in the here-and-now and the future, animating the faces and bodies and hearts of the people I worship with. For better or worse, this is what I expect, and what I respond to, in the work I now do as a Unitarian Universalist minister. Some would say this is a Generation X phenomenon. The aesthetic and the emotive are strong aspects of the way we relate to the world. Raised on MTV and the sound bite, we may not have the attention span of our parents and grandparents, but we know what it feels like to be engaged with all of our senses. I crave that kind of engagement when I go to church.

Much has been written about Generation X in the last decade. Having spent most of our lives overshadowed by our parents, the Baby Boomers who dramatically outrank us in numbers and influence, we started getting some attention as we hit our 20s and began moving into the adult world. We emerged from the financial prosperity of the 1980s expecting to keep riding the winds of an economy that, with the exception of a blip in the late 1970s and early 1980s, had grown unceasingly since the end of World War II. We expected to slip seamlessly into the privileges and securities that our parents had enjoyed. But by the 1990s, when we tried to claim our inheritance, many were disappointed. I was no exception. I graduated from university straight into the recession of the mid-1990s and the stagflation that followed it. Our generation felt the full thrust of corporate downsizing and the transfer of many entry-level positions into the developing world. We knew we were in trouble. I escaped the specter of minimum-wage dead-end work by returning to graduate school. Many of my friends, less inclined to accumulate more student debt, competed for low-end jobs that went nowhere. They struggled to find work that was meaningful and paid the bills (if they were lucky, maybe even more than the bills!). As we experienced these limitations and their effects firsthand, we also witnessed the explosion of the information age and the exciting possibilities that accompanied it. As the job market became more unstable, the world opened up before our eyes. Part of our identity as a generational group has involved coming to terms with this paradox: we faced the direct limitations of our world and concurrently experienced the broadening of that world through unbelievable advances in technology. Globalization is working itself out in our livelihoods.

So are significant changes in the structure of family life. We are the first generation to experience divorce on a massive scale from a child's perspective. I watched many of my friends' families dissolve, and I constantly worried about my own. We have been a generation slow to commit to marriage, often waiting until our 30s to do so. When asked why, many will tell you that we want to make sure we get married for the right reasons and that we want to be financially secure before we do. None of us want to go through what our parents did, or to see our kids to experience what many in our generation did.

It is difficult to find a defining moment for our generation—an event we can look back on and say, "Oh yes, there it is." We never had collective generational rites of passage like the Depression, World War II, Stonewall, Woodstock, or Vietnam, although we are saturated in their nostalgia and often mistake the theatricality surrounding them for the real thing. Perhaps the one thing that had the possibility of making us a "we" generation was AIDS. We came of age in the decade when AIDS was first recognized for what it was. We are the first generation in a century for whom sex has had a clear connection with death. We have no memory of free love. That was for those who preceded us. We watched condom machines enter our schools, our dormitories, and our bars and dance clubs, and many of us are horrified to see them now being removed by unrealistic abstinence-only agendas. But somehow even the AIDS scare didn't unite us as a generation. It was easy to marginalize the epidemic to a certain segment of society. Perhaps the extent to which we self-define as individuals and as consumers was too strong to override in the face of AIDS. We Gen-Xers have been taught that it's all about us.

I am aware that one cannot define an entire generation so simply. There are most certainly differences that arise through gender, race, class, sexual orientation, religion, and culture. My experience is grounded in my femaleness, my whiteness, my queerness, my graduate education, my upbringing in a Canadian Russian Mennonite immigrant community with its collective cultural memory of persecution, and a class tension rooted in the perpetual financial hardship of our farming family desperately hoping for a middle-class security that constantly eluded us. Furthermore, my generation of Russian Mennonites (mostly third-generation immigrants) are increasingly separated from our originating culture. We watched our parents rebel against their immigrant parents with beer and the Beatles. We took that rebellion one step further. Many of us simply melted into North American norms and attitudes.

From this personal grounding, I have observed these Gen-X tendencies in myself and others of my generation. We tend to be realists. A great many of us are cynics. Our generation is very presentist. We live for ourselves, and we live in the moment. Many of my generation are reconciled to the reality of work that may not be as meaningful as hoped, as well-paid as expected, or as stable as needed. It may be a risk even to articulate that we want more out of life. Even our efforts at individualism have been tapped into as a mass market and sold back to us. It is a kind of individualism that separates us from one another by promoting personal autonomy at all costs.

The challenge of our generation is to find hope and to practice love in this reality that promotes this kind of individualism. Our challenge is to rise from that Sunday-school basement and to take our place as adults in the sanctuary of life, seeing in the minute movements of our lives the creation of the sacred. Our calling is to move from our disparate moments and to rise as one, hearing in the roar of the floor beneath our feet the movements of the divine, our voices united, rising above the pragmatism and cynicism that tempt us from within and without. For our generation, it is truly countercultural to stand up for hope, love, and optimism.

As I look back over the few years in which I have had the privilege to minister in our living religious tradition, I wonder how my Gen-X experience is shaping the ministry I do. The first wave of us have made our way into the ministry, and as with any generation claiming its place, we have a forming edge. We are translating our experience into a larger ministry meant to deepen the faith of those we serve and to strengthen the institutions within which we work. Like the contributions of all generations, ours both emerges from our rich tradition and challenges it. Our contribution is emerging from our unique experience, one of disappointment coupled with possibility, one of pessimism and realism combined with a strong desire to reclaim hope, joy, and idealism.

The Gen-X experience has led to some particular spiritual yearnings: a hunger for relevance and true value, a hunger to reconnect with the experience of humility, a deep need to reclaim selflessness and sacrifice as meaningful and necessary, and a hunger for certainty. These yearnings seem to be more acute among Gen-Xers but are not limited to this group. After all, the generations preceding us have grown up through the world that we grew up in. Certain spiritual yearnings have surprised me because they are so countercultural. I am surprised to find them in myself, and surprised to discover that they also resonate in others.

The hunger for relevance and true value emerges from a society that is filled with transitory images and a lack of meaning. We are saturated with advertising, groomed for consumerism, and trained to fulfill our slightest wish and desire. One of the side effects of this consumerism is a deep distrust of everything we see and the assumption that what we see is not the truth but rather a creation of marketing and packaging designed to get us to do something. We have a deep hunger to connect with something that has enduring relevance and value, something that matters in a deeply significant way, that rises above the meaning of a transaction, that is free from spin and image. People come into our churches in search of that relevance and true value because our churches symbolize something enduring, something that predates many of the changes we now live with. Gen-Xers in particular come to church because it represents something that existed before us and before the massive changes we have witnessed. Many of us come for tradition; we come for ritual; we come for something to take us out of our cynical mindset. We come to hear the roaring in the floor, and we desperately want to believe that it is not just a special effect generated for our momentary entertainment, but rather the moving of a powerful presence greater than anything.

In a culture that has predisposed us to believe that we are the center of our personal universes, we are hungering to reconnect with the experience of humility. I am seeing deep inside many people the need to be decentered from that center. We have been taught that it's all about us, but something deep inside is saying, "No. There is more." We may not know how to articulate that insight; we may have no clue how to go about decentering from that center; but the desire is there, waiting to be identified and recognized. This quest is profoundly about reshaping our sense of identity from self-service to service for something greater than ourselves. Many come into our churches barely aware of this need. They come into our churches for themselves, because they are hungry and often are not sure what they hunger for. Sometimes it is that consumerist impulse that brings them, that need to respond quickly to the most recent desire. Inevitably, those who come for quick fulfillment will be disappointed in our churches. The consumer impulses that have been cultivated in us cannot be met in our churches, nor should they be. Once the first major disappointment has occurred, some people will leave, unable to rise higher than their latest whims or curiosities. But others will stay. These are the people who have the ability for that decentering and the willingness to move beyond that first disappointment, people who hunger for a humility that opens then up to a deeper way of living. Then, the hunger for decentering becomes more apparent and reveals the need for a dramatic change in self-identity and self-image.

We have a poignant need to reclaim selflessness and sacrifice as deeply meaningful. Whereas humility is about self-identity and self-image, selflessness and sacrifice are about manifesting that self-image in the way life is lived. I can recall once discussing with volunteers the approach we should use in a particular church communication. One volunteer who had experience in advertising suggested that we avoid the word "sacrifice" because it would turn people off. I suggested that we turn that thinking on its head. We are not here to reaffirm the self-centeredness of the culture around us. We are about something profoundly different. Surprisingly, the suggestion was welcomed across the board, and the concept of sacrifice became a pivotal image for us.

The hunger for sacrifice is a response to a growing weariness with self-indulgence and a greater awareness of its cost. Unfettered self-indulgence has produced people who are profoundly out of touch with themselves and with their world. In our isolation we are increasingly unaffected by the suffering of others, and thus unable to touch our own deepest places. This inability has left a spiritual void, one that can easily be taken advantage of. Fundamentalist churches have come to understand that void quite well and in responding to it have reaped the benefits; their churches are filled to overflowing. They are not afraid to ask for sacrifice, understanding it to be the pivotal element in moving through and out of that isolation. Liberal churches like ours, more in the grip of self-centeredness, have taken longer to learn and likely still have much to learn. We fear that asking for sacrifice will send people out the door, that it will compromise our freedom. Our commitment to individualism, not unlike the larger society's, has often been the kind of individualism that promotes complete autonomy. We have often, in the way we express our freedom, created exactly the void that is stripping our lives of a sacred purpose. The Gen-X hunger for enduring value offers a way out of this cycle. We are increasingly ready to ask for sacrifice, and those searching for a meaningful faith practice are more and more hungry to be asked to sacrifice something, anything, so that we can reconnect to the beating of our hearts.

We hunger for certainty amid the reality of unending transformation and change. I can feel it in myself and am not surprised in the least that other colleagues of mine see it in their Gen-Xers. Change is such an unending reality in our lives, and we have been groomed to accept this change as normal, inevitable, something to be welcomed even as we grieve what is being lost. We come to church looking for something that will stand still amid the changes around us. It's not that we want our churches to be archaic remnants of a nostalgic, seemingly peaceful and seamless world. That's just more campiness. Many come to our churches wanting something to hold on to that they can trust will remain there for them. Part of this longing is a search for definition. They want to know what we believe, what we stand for, and what it all means. When I meet with prospective members, chances are that the Gen-Xers are looking for more certainty than anyone else. They want answers more than they want questions. Hymns like "The Question Is the Answer" feel hollow to them. Who can blame them? We live in times of unbelievable change, and there is a deep hunger in our society for certainty. Is it any wonder that religions offering clear answers are raking in the converts? The people who come to Unitarian Universalism are unlikely to want black-and-white answers, but they do want answers nonetheless. They want some refuge from the uncertainty of their personal lives, their work lives, and their lives as citizens of this country in flux. We are "the church of the question" and often fall short of the mark when approached by Gen-Xers wanting something more.

These hungers and yearnings—for relevance and value, humility, selflessness and sacrifice, and certainty—have deep repercussions for how we do Unitarian Universalism. In a religious tradition that has trumpeted freedom and individualism as its spiritual hallmarks, our churches respond with difficulty to the hunger for humility and sacrifice. In a religious tradition that sees truth as always changing and the practice of faith as a process, we are being asked to respond to the deep spiritual need for constancy and reassurance. In a religious tradition that gives power to relativity, Gen-Xers are pulling us out of that comfortable place of no answers and asking us to impart the truth and something of clear, lasting value. The yearnings for relevance and value, humility, selflessness, and sacrifice challenge many of the ways that Unitarian Universalists have come to self-identify.

For many Gen-Xers, it no longer feels enough to identify Unitarian Universalism as the religion that stands for freedom and individualism. While intellectually this definition is powerful and true, it rings, for many like myself, with a certain faddish hollowness. As a product of the "I" generation, as a Gen-Xer who has been force-fed consumerist individualism, I find that when Unitarian Universalists hold up the primacy of the individual, I feel cynicism and doubt. I know intellectually that the freedom of our faith is exactly what brought me to it. There is a reason I no longer attend a Mennonite church—there was not enough freedom to be who I was. I know that the work of freedom-loving Unitarians, Universalists, and Unitarian Universalists created this wonderful religion I serve. But I have seen too many Unitarian Universalist churches fall into petty selfishness and insularity, all in the name of freedom, for me to feel completely comfortable with an emphasis on freedom. Moreover, I cannot forget what it was like to watch many of my friends' families fall apart as their parents claimed the need for personal freedom and self-actualization, a key hallmark of identity for the Baby-Boomer generation. In saying this, my intention is not to judge those who chose the path of divorce, but I experienced its impact as a child. I constantly feared the end of my parents' marriage as I watched my friends' families fall apart. Divorce has indelibly marked my generation. For all these reasons and more, I get nervous when our churches hold up the commitment to individual freedom and self-actualization as the hallmark of our faith. Self-actualization is not a sufficient foundation upon which to build and sustain a life-giving, love-saturated religious community. There must be more.

My doubts about the primacy of individualism and the centrality of freedom have profoundly influenced my ministry. I have increasingly emphasized responsibility: the responsible use of freedom, the responsible use of knowledge, the responsible use of our individual gifts and talents. The assumption of responsibility has more often been the focus of my developing theology than the exercise of freedom. I emphasize the collective as much as, if not more than, the individual. I encourage the congregations I serve to feel the needs of the other as keenly as if they were their own.

By way of example, the congregation I now serve made some significant decisions last year regarding how we do worship. At first, the proposed changes met with considerable and expected resistance. At the initial congregational consultation, the conversation emphasized the personal impact of the proposed changes. People talked about what they themselves wanted in worship and measured their support of the changes by their perception of how well the changes would meet their individual needs. I encouraged them to go deeper. Individual needs were a good starting place, but if that was the extent of our deliberation, we had missed the mark. We needed to go beyond ourselves and consider as much, if not more, the impact of the proposal on the entire worshiping community, including those who had not found us yet. Most important, support for the changes should be measured not by individual fulfillment of needs but by the fulfillment of our larger vision.

We needed to move beyond ourselves and to be true stewards of our message of love, freedom, and responsibility. The next congregational meeting had a very different tone. The focus shifted away from competing individual needs to a sense of moving together in a common direction. The congregation unanimously approved the changes at the annual congregational meeting. Clearly, the future of our faith depends on a sensitive decentering of the individual so that we can make strong choices and deep offerings of love and compassion to the world around us.

X X X

For many Gen-Xers, it no longer feels sufficient to affirm Unitarian Universalism as the religion that trusts in the inherent goodness of humanity, another cornerstone of our faith tradition. My ministry is dramatically affected by my own doubts about this inherent goodness. So often our emphasis on our inherent goodness feels to me like self-congratulation and a way to avoid taking responsibility for the evil we do, even if unintended. It allows us to lay a gloss over the complexity and intricacy of the human experience. I do not wish to turn away from the power of this concept. Unitarian Universalism offers a profoundly different kind of healing salvation to those deeply damaged by churches offering only an understanding of humanity as depraved. However, I think we have underestimated and failed to respond pastorally and theologically to our potential for evil. Perhaps I am not so different from those disaffected liberal Christians in the 1920s, so demoralized by the atrocities of World War I that many sought refuge in a renewed orthodoxy. I see so much potential for harm in our nature, in the way we manage fear and anxiety, and in our difficulty seeing beyond our prideful, selfish desires. My ministry responds to this darkness perhaps as much as our Unitarian and Universalist ancestors emphasized our goodness. I seek always to respond pastorally to the struggle of working through our darkness to reclaim the light within. I have found in the concept of humility one of the most effective tools we have to acknowledge the evil that we do and the evil that we could do. Humility helps us resist evil itself—the evil inside us and the evil around us—so that we may gain access to the goodness that we do have, the goodness that reaffirms the presence of God within all humanity. Humility decenters us from self-centered pride, pride often nourished by our rabid addiction to unfettered individualism, pride that keeps us from acknowledging the consequences of our actions and our potential for evil. Humility holds us in a more cautious and questioning stance toward our own internal natures. It aids us in being able to uncover when our desires are motivated by self-indulgence and when they are motivated by a true love for life. This work is especially important as our churches draw predominantly from the white middle classes whose culture and economic ability encourage self-centeredness and pridefulness—both of which so easily blind us to the consequences of our way of life has on the world around us.

What this approach means, in practice, is that I encourage those I serve to be vigilant regarding their personal desires and wants and to monitor those desires and wants for whether they emerge from a place of fear or one of love. We are free when we act out of love. We are imprisoned when we act out of fear. This is not a faith for those who want to coast through life. The practice of our faith is a discipline, one that must be consciously engaged and continually renewed. Nothing is to be taken for granted. Every moment is an opportunity through which we can choose either to close our hearts or to open them. Neither goodness nor evil emerges of its own accord. Our faith asks us, as beings with consciousness and the ability make choices, to choose wisely and to infuse everything we are and everything we do with our commitment to act always through love. I frequently recognize our failure to do this, urge forgiveness of self and forgiveness of the other for our failures, and then encourage us to try again.

X X X

Perhaps it is the Gen-X hunger for truth, value, and certainty that challenges us most of all. Unitarian Universalism is very much a faith wedded to process, with the assumption that everything changes, even truth, at some point. We are supported in our process-oriented faith by postmodernism, which posits no center to truth, but rather posits truth as wedded to context. I find great value in postmodernism and see much of use in its way of approaching the meaning we give to our lives and the world around us. It assists us in holding our absolutes lightly. It keeps us from being unbending, rigid, and prideful.

At the same time, there is a distinct difference between an intellectual and theological commitment to openness and diversity of truth, and the spiritual need for constancy and a truth that is enduring. We are much better at approaching the first than the second.

We live in a world where the cycles of social and economic change have sped up markedly. This rapid pace of change has deep spiritual and religious consequences. Our trust in ourselves, our governments, the economy, the future, science, and the ability of people to work together—all these have been shaken. Our hope that life will improve for our children is no longer a given. Postmodern life is increasingly isolated, and we are not often given the tools to enter truly into relationship with one another, let alone ourselves. If we are to respond to the religious and spiritual hungers that we experience with the rapid pace of change, we need to engage that delicate balance of remaining committed to faith as a process, while acknowledging and responding to a deep longing for something substantial to hold on to. The spiritual cost of such rapid change is high—feelings of helplessness, anger, smallness, and fear. To respond to these feelings means touching the pain and acknowledging our powerlessness. It means identifying the impact on us of the changes we have witnessed, created, abetted, resisted, and accepted.

Our challenge is to hold onto the concept of change as inevitable, change as good, while recognizing that not all change is inevitable or good. Some change is the consequence of poorly thought-out choices that have had huge repercussions for our spiritual and economic well-being. These repercussions include isolation, a deep sense of irrelevance, disempowerment, and dehumanization. I struggle in my ministry to hold onto the truth of process, the truth of relativity, while responding pastorally to these very real consequences and the needs that arise from them—the need for constancy, the need for reassurance, for something that stands still. Achieving this balance is a challenge for Unitarian Universalism. Unitarian Universalism often ends up being regarded as the practice of change for the sake of change. One of the worst things one can say to Unitarian Universalists is that they are afraid of change. Such a comment serves to delegitimize whatever position a Unitarian Universalist may hold. While there is no doubt that we need to embrace change, there are times when we must respect the deep spiritual need that rests beneath the resistance to it. Unless you address the need, no change, even good change, is possible.

One of the ways I try to respond to the need for constancy and reassurance is to resist that oft-stated truism, "The question is the answer." I have grown increasingly impatient with questions that are not followed by answers. I would much prefer a confident answer than a noncommittal question. Tell me what you think I should do! Give me something to hold on to! Point me in a direction! In the Unitarian Universalist penchant for questions that are never answered, we have often taken the coward's way out. Questions are a way to back out of taking a stand and taking the flak for that stand. They are a way to avoid conflict and a true engagement with our complex and paradoxical world, a way of staying comfortably wrapped up in irrelevance. A religion that remains safely immersed in questions stands for nothing.

Our people are searching for answers to make sense of what is happening to them. Questions left hanging do a disservice to that deep spiritual need. The answers need to involve not just factual explanations but also a deeper insight into the realm of the heart and how our souls are responding to change. There has been great pain laid upon the backs of people as the ways of the postindustrial world work themselves out in our lives. Do we have the courage to name that pain?

Up to now, we have not had that courage. We have barely touched upon the psychological and spiritual ramifications of the postindustrial age enough to respond pastorally to the realities of our parishioners' lives. To respond means speaking the truth of what has happened to many of our people. It means acknowledging that some in our congregations have risen to new heights of affluence while others have fallen behind. To respond means affirming feelings of helplessness, anger, smallness, and fear. To respond means touching the pain and acknowledging the many ways in which we are powerless. To respond means recognizing the losses, speaking to the loneliness and dislocation, and addressing the frustration. And it means holding up something that is much greater, much more powerful, and much truer than anything else—the power of love. This is our constant, and the role of our churches is to release it in ourselves, in each other, and in our world. Whether that means offering comfort or having the courage to make each other extremely uncomfortable, that's what it is about. It is about releasing a love that in all its complexity, paradox, and simplicity is begging to be given away.

The Gen-X spiritual yearnings for constancy, reassurance, comfort, and answers, along with decentering and sacrifice, are this generation's contributions to the calling that our churches have served since they first burst forth from the wailings of a burning Servetus—the release of love and compassion in ourselves and in the world. This is what our hungers are about. When we hunger for relevance and true value, when we hunger for sacrifice and humility, when we hunger for constancy and reassurance, this is what we are responding to, that age-old calling to be filled with love and compassion so that we may be beacons of light in a world struggling to move through paradox and unpredictability.

When God shook the floor of Oak Street United Mennonite Church, I thought anything was possible. I waited for the day that I would witness this power and possibility firsthand. What a lesson it was to realize that it was not simply there for the taking. I pray that we will assume our place in that sanctuary, that our rising and sitting ricochets through that old wooden floor. May our voices thunder through the pregnant air with sincerity of purpose. As our children listen to us, children who have not yet doubted the majesty and grandeur that emanate from our conscious and unconscious choices, may they approach our thin, indiscernible words and hear in them the Truth. May our sanctuaries, and our hearts, be filled with the hunger for truth, value, hope, healing, purpose, and renewal. And may those hungers release us into love and compassion so that we may be ready to serve our waiting and impatient world. Amen.

A SEAT AT THE COMMAND TABLE

DAVID PYLE

I am a U.S. Army veteran and have served as a special operations soldier and a paratrooper in both Latin America and Bosnia-y-Herzegovina. Much of my faith as a Unitarian Universalist is rooted in the experience of my military service, and it is fitting that through my Unitarian Universalist faith I have discovered a way that I can once again be in military service.

Having grown up in a family that was conservative both politically and religiously, I had my childhood assumptions shaken by my encounters with poverty and anger in Latin America. Serving as a peacekeeper in Bosnia after the Dayton Peace Accords were signed transformed my understanding of the costs of war, not in terms of dollars but in terms of lives and societies. My time in Bosnia also brought me face to face with the evil that we humans can visit upon each other and with the hatred that fuels that evil.

It may be no surprise then that when I began the path to the ministry, the call to military chaplaincy spoke to me, especially when I learned how few Unitarian Universalist ministers were serving as military chaplains at that time.

While I was wrestling with the decision to apply to seminary—and considering putting my uniform back on—I had the pleasure of meeting the Rev. Bill Sinkford in Houston. He had preached a sermon on the good news of Unitarian Universalism; standing in the receiving line, I wondered if I would say anything to him about my call. When it was my turn to shake his hand, a friend of mine announced to everyone around that I was applying to seminary and that I wanted to become a military chaplain.

Bill Sinkford smiled and told me that his son, who at that time was serving as an Army ranger in Afghanistan, called him once a month or so to ask why there were so few UU ministers serving as military chaplains. I had been worried about what kind of support I might receive in seeking military ministry, and I was elated to find support in the person of the UUA president. We talked for about five minutes, and then I allowed the line to move on.

Floating on clouds, I walked back to my table. I realize now that the conversation with Bill Sinkford had been overheard by several people, but I was unaware of that at the time—until a young woman stopped me.

The first thing I noticed was her necklace: a pendant with a chalice superimposed on a peace sign hanging on a long leather cord. Without any preamble or introduction she said, "I don't see how you can call yourself a UU and be willing to serve in the military."

There are times in life when something speaks through you, when what needs to be said is said before you even realize you are going to speak. Without a second's thought I looked at her and said, "How can we expect the military to show our Unitarian Universalist values and ideals if we aren't willing to be there?"

I never met this woman again, and I'm not certain I would recognize her if I did. Yet as she turned around and walked away from me, I realized that the call to serve our faith as a military chaplain is not just about serving as a religious counselor to service members. It is about serving our nation as an ethical voice within the ranks of our military. It is about defending the free exercise of religion for service members. It is about serving our association as a bridge between ourselves and those who serve in uniform. The young woman who challenged my call saw that distance as unbridgeable, but I knew it was not, for it had been bridged within my own heart and soul.

If it were not for my time in uniform when I was in my early 20s, I would not be a Unitarian Universalist today. I felt the power of transformation the first time a Panamanian woman showed me her home, a small cinderblock room with a tin roof and a dirt floor that she shared with eight other people. I felt the power of transformation on the day in Bosnia when I realized that the warehouse with bullet holes and broken glass that we were using for storage and offices had begun its life not as a warehouse, but as the Sarajevo Winter Olympics Ice Skating Arena. I felt the power of transformation on the day that a sweet, grandmotherly Bosnian Muslim woman had an earnest conversation with me about the necessity of the genocide of the Bosnian Serbs.

These experiences and others brought me to realize that our world is much more complex than I had ever dreamt. I began to see that my views of the world and how to be in relationship to it were too simplistic, too focused on placing the world in boxes of us-versus-them. These experiences placed me on the path of seeking a different way for humans to live together, a path that brought me to Unitarian Universalism. It was these experiences that brought me to understand the inherent worth and dignity of every person, and to see the interdependent web of all existence. None of these experiences would have come to me had I not served in the military, and I am not alone in this kind of transformation.

Since beginning the path to ministry, I have had the pleasure of visiting and speaking at over a dozen Unitarian Universalist congregations in four states, and in those congregations I found fellow veterans sitting in the pews, many of whom had discovered the transformational experiences of their own Unitarian Universalist faith during their time in uniform. In some congregations I found active-duty service members who felt, as I do, that their military service and their Unitarian Universalist values were bound together, inseparable, for the one arose from the other. One man I met is now a pacifist because of his experiences as a soldier in Vietnam; another changed his views of women because of his experiences in Desert Storm. In many of these congregations, I found fear among veterans and service members that if they were too public about their experiences, thoughts, and feelings, they would no longer be welcome in this church they had come to love.

In my conversations with those veterans I saw, I believe, the first purpose of military chaplaincy within our religious movement. By an associational commitment to support an increasing number of military chaplains, we say to those UUs who are currently serving: We recognize your presence among us, and we recognize your need for spiritual support. We recognize that the military is not a monolith of conservative religious views, and we commit to welcoming you as valued members of our movement of religious liberalism and of our congregations. By such a commitment, we raise awareness in our own congregations of the need to support not only those members of our faith serving in uniform, but also to support their families who are so often left behind.

Such an associational commitment to support an increasing number of military chaplains also says to the veterans sitting quietly in our pews that it is OK to share their experiences. By affirming that people can serve in the military and still be Unitarian Universalists, we allow them the space necessary to begin sharing their stories, joys, and sorrows with us, experiences that I believe will make us a deeper and richer religious tradition. Perhaps more importantly, we will allow some of them the space they need to take the next step in healing from some of the traumatic experiences of their own military service.

On one occasion I was sitting in the pews of a UU congregation in Chicago, attending a Sunday-morning service. While waiting for the service to begin, I began chatting with the man sitting next to me. When he asked why I was visiting Chicago, I told him I was a student at a local seminary. He then asked where I wanted to be a minister when I graduated, and I mentioned to him that I was working toward military chaplaincy.

As he sat back, looking surprised, I steeled myself for another discussion about whether or not UUs should be allowed to serve in the military, but he surprised me. He told me that he did not know there were any UU ministers serving as military chaplains, and then quietly said he wished he had known one when he was in Vietnam. As we talked, I learned that as a combat infantryman in Vietnam he had been called on to kill, and the guilt of that experience had been with him ever since. He had attended Unitarian Universalist services for years but had never joined a congregation because he did not feel worthy. He had never told anyone in a UU church about his military service, fearing that this church he needed so badly would be taken away. Coming to services, attending protests against war, and sitting quietly in the pews were for him penance. He just never felt that he could speak about his experiences; instead he suffered in silence.

Our military chaplains serve our association as a reminder that we do value those who serve or have served our nation, even if we do not always agree with what they are called to do. It is a statement that we value the individual's inherent worth and dignity at the same time that we wish for humankind to find other ways to resolve our conflicts. By committing ourselves to increasing the number of military chaplains who are Unitarian Universalists and by being public in our support for them as they serve, we tell those veterans, service members, and their families that they and their experiences are welcome and valuable parts of our congregations. In so doing, we also provide a vital service for those service members who are not Unitarian Universalists, for our lived faith is well suited to serving the religious diversity that exists in the military. The purpose of the military chaplaincy is to defend the constitutional right to the free exercise of religion, something enshrined in the heart of Unitarian Universalism.

When I began the process to be accepted as a U.S. Army second lieutenant and a chaplaincy candidate, my recruiter told me that he had trouble finding ministers who were willing to provide care for people outside their own faith tradition without evangelizing to them. After a little research into our faith, he did not think that would be a problem for Unitarian Universalists.

I mentioned that historically both the Unitarians and the Universalists have been deeply involved in military chaplaincy, and that the founder of American Universalism, John Murray, served as George Washington's chaplain during the American Revolution.

A military chaplain is not assigned to minister only to those of his or her faith tradition. With duties similar to those of a hospital chaplain, a military chaplain is assigned to a unit, ship, installation or squadron. A chaplain will find service members of many different religious traditions within the unit he or she is assigned to and must minister to them all. Whatever chaplains cannot perform, they are required to provide. They care for all.

In military ministry, your faith is a personal source of strength to be with service members and their families through both the best and the worst of times. A chaplain's faith is the hope that he or she brings to the door with a notification officer to be with a spouse who learns that a loved one will not be coming home again. A chaplain's faith is the love that sustains him or her in personal moments of despair, when consoling a group of marines who have just lost their gunnery sergeant in combat. A chaplain's faith is the courage that calls him or her to be wherever needed, sometimes within the hell of war itself. A chaplain's faith is not what he or she seeks to convert another to, unless invited to do so by the other person.

Chaplain (Lt.) Cynthia Kane, a UU minister serving as a Navy chaplain, once said to me that while serving as a chaplain aboard a U.S. Navy aircraft carrier, very few of the sailors she ministered to would have known that she was a Unitarian Universalist, because her personal faith was secondary to her identity as "Chaps" among her sailors. Her faith is vitally important to her, in that it is the strength, hope, love and courage to be there with her sailors, "coasties" (members of the Coast Guard), and marines. To those she served with, it was much more important that she was the chaplain, no matter what tradition she came from.

My own life and service have been touched several times by military chaplains, and in all but one case I have no idea what religious traditions they came from. The chaplain who most touched my life was my unit chaplain when my father passed away. In March of 1994 I was a member of the Seventh Special Forces Group (Airborne) based at Fort Bragg, North Carolina, but I was temporarily assigned to the U.S. Embassy in San Salvador, El Salvador. My family had no way to contact me directly because of my mission's security requirements when my father died unexpectedly of a heart attack.

My father was my best friend and my hero, an Army veteran himself.

When I joined the military, I went into almost the same field he did. When news came that he was gone, I was shaken to the bedrock of my life.

My mother called my first sergeant, and my first sergeant called our unit chaplain. At six o'clock the following morning, I received a call from my first sergeant telling me that I needed to call my mother. After that call, in which my mother told me my dad had passed away, I called my first sergeant back, and he set up a three-way call with our unit chaplain. The chaplain had already been on the phone with the Embassy's Deputy Consulate of Mission (DCM) and had already received approval for my mission to be put on hold and for me to head home. Over the next two hours, my chaplain and the DCM made phone calls on my behalf. Two people were bumped off of a flight out of El Salvador so that I could be on it. The chaplain made sure that someone would travel with me so that I did not have to be alone. At customs in Miami, an airport official met me and rushed me through to my next flight. In Atlanta, a flight was held on the ground for 15 minutes so that I could board. When I landed in Nashville, a former minister of my family church picked me up at the airport and drove me to my mother's home in Knoxville, Tennessee.

It was early morning when I learned of my father's passing, and by ten o'clock that night I was hugging my mother and my sisters. To this day I do not know who paid for my plane tickets. The following day a unit chaplain for the National Guard unit in Knoxville called to check on me, and so did my own chaplain back at Fort Bragg. At the time I was lost in my own grief, but looking back, I see that my chaplain made sure that the military and the embassy knew I had to be released to go home. He made sure that I would make it home in time for the funeral, and he had a chaplain who was nearby check on me and my family once I was home. To this day I have no idea if my chaplain was a Roman Catholic, a Baptist, or a Buddhist. In the end, it does not matter. He was my chaplain.

There is also a growing movement of Unitarian Universalism within the military. Unitarian Universalist congregations around major military bases find that significant portions of their membership are serving, have served, or are related to the military. Unitarian Universalists who are serving in the military overseas often affiliate with the Church of the Larger Fellowship, and in one case that I know of in Germany they have formed their own UU congregation. I believe that it is possible in the near future that fellowship model congregations may begin to form on U.S. military bases. Unitarian Universalist chaplains are also able to serve with authenticity religious traditions such as Wicca and Ásatrú, which are not represented in the military chaplaincy corps, and can help to educate fellow chaplains about them.

No matter how wonderful a chaplain is, there are times when service members need to speak with a minister within, or familiar with, their own tradition. No matter how wonderful a civilian minister is, there are also times a soldier needs to speak to someone who understands the military and the special issues that life as a service member entails—and who has had the same kinds of experiences.

For example, about two years ago, a young sergeant in the U.S. Air Force contacted me through the internet because he was looking for a Unitarian Universalist military chaplain. He was seeking counsel on whether becoming more public about his sexual orientation was worth the risk to his military career. He wondered whether hiding his being gay had ethical implications that related to his Unitarian Universalist faith. Unable to find a UU chaplain, he contacted me to see if I could help. At the time, I could not contact any of our ministers serving as military chaplains either, and as a friend he and I talked about his life under the "don't ask, don't tell" policy. He knew that a UU minister would protect his confidence, but he was not assured that his chaplain would. He knew his chaplain would understand the importance of his military career, but he was not assured that a UU minister would.

We must have Unitarian Universalist military chaplains to support the members of our religious movement serving in uniform. Our chaplains—as well as former and retired military chaplains and other veterans—can serve our congregations as advocates for veterans and military families in our churches. Finding ways to connect current and former military chaplains with UU service members, veterans, and families is vital to the spiritual health of our faith.

We also need to have the courage to admit that, as a religious movement, we have not always welcomed those who combine their Unitarian Universalist faith with the calling to serve in uniform. At a meeting of UUs affiliated with the military at the 2005 General Assembly in Fort Worth, Texas, veterans, military families, and currently serving soldiers, sailors, airmen and marines came together to share stories about what it is like to be a UU in the military. In one case, a marine spoke of how letting other UUs at a leadership conference know that he was a major in the Marine Corps led to others shunning him for the remainder of the conference. Another shared how he had never told anyone in his church that he had served in Vietnam, and one woman talked of how, while her husband was serving in Iraq, she received little emotional, spiritual, or physical support from members of her church—and some had even questioned her faith and that of her husband. Being a UU and a service member can make one feel like something of an outsider, both in the military and in the church.

Vietnam taught us better ways of treating veterans, but we must not stop at merely refraining from ridiculing them. We as a movement of religious liberalism need to learn to support those who serve, support the families of those who serve, and care for veterans when they return. We can do this at the same time we oppose the wars our government chooses to fight. By doing both, we gain authenticity in each effort, and we better care for wounded, frightened, and hurting members of our congregations as well.

For change to happen within any institution, and for the desire for change to find grounding and traction, it must have supporters both within and outside of the institution. If we feel that the military needs to be brought more into tune with our Unitarian Universalist values and ideals, then advocating for such change from outside the military is simply not enough. Such advocacy, without deep connections within the military, is often based more upon our ideals and less upon practical reality. Such outside advocacy is necessary, even vital, to promoting social justice within the military, but alone it is not enough.

Our military chaplains serve Unitarian Universalist ideals in three vital ways. First, they and our UU veterans and service members are the voices of experience within our movement on what life and policy are like within the military, and are vital in formulating strategies on how to work toward achieving our goals of social justice. They can see, often better than anyone outside the military culture, where the true social injustices within the military lie, and how they can best be addressed by our association.

Second, our military chaplains make the same commitment to the military that all other service members make. They take the same oath of office that all military officers take, and they take that oath just as seriously. When an issue is raised by a military chaplain who is also a fellow officer, it gets a different reception than it would if raised from a picket line outside the gates of a military base. A military chaplain would not make it through training or through a term of service without having love and respect for his or her fellow service members. When something is said by a chaplain, it is said in love by a comrade. Such voices are vital if we are truly to work for justice within the policies and practices of our military.

Our military chaplains are also there with the soldiers and their officers when tactical and strategic decisions are made. Soldiers and officers are taught that, when you have an ethical quandary, or when an issue weighs on your heart and soul, one of the people that you can go to for advice and counsel is your chaplain. In every unit I have served, the commanding officers met regularly with the unit chaplain on issues of morale and ethics. In one unit, the chaplain even helped teach Officer Professional Development classes on ethics. If there were ever a place where we as Unitarian Universalists need to have our voices heard, it is seated at the command table.

There are also social justice issues within our current military that need to be addressed, and our military chaplains are in a position to have a positive effect on the lives of individual service members and families. Many men and women who join the military are from disadvantaged backgrounds and are seeking opportunities for education and advancement. Their families back home may have financial or health needs, and military chaplains are able to help service members discover ways to help their families. Within our military there are also people who have been marginalized, sometimes for their sexual orientation or religious preferences. These people need the kind of welcoming ministry that Unitarian Universalist chaplains provide while keeping their confidence. Chaplains often serve as powerful advocates for the marginalized. Chaplain (Capt.) George Tyger, a UU minister serving in the Army, told me that our faith tradition also should serve the Chaplaincy Corps itself by keeping watch that the purpose of the military chaplaincy remains the protection of the free exercise of religion in the military.

Combat operations and changing economic situations can present seemingly insurmountable challenges to a spouse who is left behind to work, manage a household, and care for children during a deployment. Beyond meeting the need for spiritual ministry to those families, the chaplain is in a position to see and understand their physical needs, and to help those families find the support they need.

In this way, military chaplaincy is a social justice ministry, one that can connect deeply with the lives of many who would probably never sit in the pews of our congregations. This integrated understanding of military chaplaincy—including social justice, pastoral counseling, and ethical action—is something I believe Unitarian Universalist ministers serving as military chaplains would excel at. We bring the good news of Unitarian Universalism to the lives of people in a way other evangelism might not. As we claim to be a faith of deeds, not creeds, serving as a military chaplain is also to serve as a missionary for our faith.

There is still the question, however, that the young woman asked me at the advertising event in Houston: "How can you call yourself a UU and be willing to serve in the military?" I stand by the answer I gave to her that day, that without UUs serving in the military our armed forces will never be more in tune with our UU ideals. Yet that is not all of my answer.

For me, the most important answer I can give to that question is love—not a love of war, for war is the only form of hell that I still believe in. No, the love I feel is for those women and men who, as the fourth stanza of our National Anthem puts it, shall stand between their loved homes and the war's desolation. They do not choose what wars to fight; we do that—we civilians and the politicians we elect.

No, these young men and women often place themselves in harm's way not for ideals but for us, for each other, and for the family members they leave behind. I have a huge place in my heart for them. Whether their service makes the world more or less safe does not change the spiritual, physical, and social costs paid by service members and their families. Whether or not we support how the military is used does not lessen our responsibility to those service members and their families. When we oppose a conflict in which someone fought and died, perhaps we are even more responsible—because we did not do enough to prevent it.

After all the arguments I have made as to why our movement of religious liberalism should support an increasing number of military chaplains, love is the one that means the most to me. It is true that there is a need for this kind of specialized ministry in the lives of the veterans, service members, and their families who come into our congregations. It is true that by serving as military chaplains, we are living the ideals of our faith through deeds and not creeds. It is true that by serving as military chaplains, we can place liberal, ethical voices where they can have input and influence on military ethics and decision making. It is true that by supporting the formation of UU ministers as military chaplains, we are able to be involved in practical ways in the many social justice issues that exist within our nation's military. All of this is true, and yet for me it is all secondary.

It is secondary to the love I feel for those young men and women in uniform, and to those who were once young and still serve. That love I feel is my core understanding of my call to military chaplaincy. Chaplain Cynthia Kane calls military chaplaincy the largest young adult ministry in the UUA, and she's right.

So my final answer to that young woman's question, "How can you call yourself a UU and be willing to serve in the military?" is that my Unitarian Universalist faith itself calls me to military ministry. How could I not serve, if and however I am able, and remain true to my faith? My faith requires that I accept a seat at the command table.

A FAITH THAT BELIEVES IN ITSELF

SHANA LYNNGOOD

I have learned many unique and fascinating things by virtue of serving a congregation in Washington, D.C. Rather than being starstruck by celebrities as those in Los Angeles often are, in the nation's capital we are awash in pundits and politicians and journalists. In a few brief years, I have run across a great many of them. It was, however, exceptional to be invited, as I was by a member of my church one summer evening, to an event with Senator Barack Obama. That's how I found myself at a posh law firm on K Street in a one-on-one conversation with the charismatic junior senator from Illinois. As I was introduced to Senator Obama by my congregant, he shook my hand and said with a wry smile on his face, "Aren't you a little young to be a pastor?" To which I replied, "Aren't you hearing the same thing as a first-year senator from many of your colleagues who have enjoyed long and powerful tenures in the Senate?" He confirmed that this was indeed the case, and we shared a laugh.

My conversation with Senator Obama isn't the only time that my age and, by extension, my wisdom and preparedness for ministry have been questioned. I have had similar conversations many times over. While I suppose that I expected this reaction when I entered the ranks of ordained colleagues at the age of 28, it has never failed to catch me off guard in its shortsightedness. While the accrual of life experience brings with it some gravitas and a greater knowledge base, it is clear to me that every generation of ministry has a vantage point and an analysis of our movement to offer that is critical to seeing the whole. To see ministry and Unitarian Universalism in a way that is clear-eyed but not jaded, and to temper cynicism with a profound belief in the transformative power of our faith, is our calling as religious leaders in our movement regardless of age.

As a lifelong Unitarian Universalist, I find that I am continually disappointed (though unfortunately not surprised) by the myriad ways we seem to be able to shoot ourselves in the foot. Riven by internal squabbles of little ultimate consequence, we seem determined to remain virtually irrelevant on the American religious landscape. While there are no doubt colleagues and laity who wish to take the legacy of our forebears seriously enough to make a difference in the lives of many more people, this will happen only if we don't need to continually explain and cajole those already in our midst who would rather continue to split hairs. How long must we have redundant conversations about the importance of our ability to use spiritual language, and the obvious reality that we must become a richly multicultural faith in order to live up to our tenets of belief before we act? As valuable as these conversations are for those who feel unclear about this larger purpose of our religion, such conversations should not keep those of us who have long since accepted these callings from moving ahead. Each time I feel that our push toward inclusion, toward living into the fullness of the "inherent worth and dignity" of all people, is obscured—obscured by our need to rehash debates of spirituality vs. humanism, or congregational polity vs. clergy authority, or social justice vs. inward community building—I am saddened. How much has been lost and how much time has been wasted on placating factions within our movement? We need to come to grips with the fact that although there are aspects of our movement on which we don't have universal agreement, we can no longer allow them to hold us back.

Throughout my time in seminary we were warned of the diminishing returns of ministry. We were told that at the rate at which mainline Protestant churches were dying, and Unitarian Universalist churches were maintaining the status quo in membership numbers, there would be little institution left to serve. We were following a vocational leading that might not take us very far. Religion and churchgoing may have mattered a great deal to my grandparents' generation, but around the country many nearly empty, architecturally exquisite buildings our forebears helped create are evidence that this is no longer the case (of course, we have witnessed simultaneously a surprising rise in the popularity of nondenominational, conservative Christian megachurches). In fact, it seems to me in retrospect that a false tension was created about the dilemma of holding onto the church as an institution with history and liturgy and tradition on the one hand, and creating communities of relevance in the daily lives of modern Americans on the other. It is clearer to me now more than ever before that we need to do both. We need to rely more heavily on the wisdom and inspired vision of our

Unitarian and Universalist forebears who took to heart the love of God and the equality and lovable state of each person—that theology is the mission for our faith. What they so eloquently articulated is exceedingly relevant and sorely lacking in contemporary American life. We have the message and mandate we need to become what we ought to be: one of the great religious traditions of our nation—a tradition that leads in vibrancy and vitality, a movement that beckons to the best in all of us to work to better our world through acts of compassion and justice because we are clear that our faith calls for nothing less. We need to stop belittling the power of our message and the capacity of our movement to reach more broadly and expansively. This work of taking the gospel of Unitarian Universalism to the streets and airwaves is where I see most clearly the contributions of those of us in the "Reverend X" generation. I see this task not so much as a new-media and internet revolution, but as a groundswell of intensity around speaking with integrity and conviction and power through our own life stories about the possibility and hope inherent in Unitarian Universalism. We still fervently believe (in a way that others perhaps have lost hope in along the way or didn't share to begin with) that ours is a faith we must live up to. There is a mantle waiting to be claimed for our association, would we but be bold enough to carry it forward.

Fervor into Action

We have for some time now said that we believe in the good news of Unitarian Universalism. Each year at General Assembly we are invited to remember this larger whole that we are a part of, and asked to see once again the potential and possibility intrinsic to who we are. Then we go back to our individual congregations and don't change a thing, or we tinker around the edges with some new fad idea about governance or membership or worship. Each year, it seems, we are convinced that something else will be the "silver bullet" that will change the dynamics. One year it is policy governance; the next it is covenants of right relationship. Much as we seem to jump from one justice issue to another year after year, we give too little concerted time and focus to our way of being, our way of offering ministry, and we spend too much time on the surfaces. After making these minor changes, we are for some reason surprised to discover that they didn't make a great deal of difference. None of these quick cosmetic fixes gets to the heart of the matter. None of these slight adjustments gets at the core shift that needs to happen if we are truly to advance. We need to stop demeaning and belittling our own faith. What we need is not some new structure or concept—we need to invest ourselves fully in the tradition we have been bequeathed. We need to live our faith and share it in a way that conveys our belief that it uniquely has much to give. In the midst of a religious landscape full of traditions that lift up the value of some over others, our tradition stands for the equality of all. In a time when religion and belief are seen as synonymous with anti-intellectualism and dislike of difference, ours is a faith that believes ardently that differences in the human family are a gift and that thoughtfulness is a virtue. If we can't believe strongly and seriously enough in what we have to offer to invite others in, then why would anyone else think our ranks are worth joining?

I am hopeful that the tide is turning. The colleagues I have met in my generation do believe. They are saying yes to offers of radio interviews and local newspaper and TV pieces—both to speak to current issues affecting their communities and to raise the profile of our movement as whole. They are getting involved in neighborhood justice issues so that we can be known for what we stand for. They are preaching theologically rich and spiritually sustaining messages that are a long way from the college-lecture-style preaching that was once widely accepted as *the* way to preach a UU sermon. They are taking seriously the desire and need for programming throughout the lifespan that speaks to how we grow spiritually, and that views helping members see the implications of leading a life rooted in Spirit as one of the critical roles of church. They are leading congregations with music programs of depth and creativity that have long since moved beyond the Western musical canon to share the beauty and soul-stirring sounds of music from all over the world and of every imaginable genre. Perhaps most critically, they have heeded the call to have church be church again. No longer content to have congregations that are social clubs or that serve in the capacity of other nonprofit justice agencies, this generation of clergy is always holding as central these questions: What makes us a church? And what difference does what we do make? It is a vantage point on ministry that makes worship more vibrant and relevant. Sermons speak to the heart as frequently as to the head, the music is soul-stirring, and the church both meets congregants where they are and challenges them to do more to improve our world.

MORE THAN SEMANTICS

It doesn't sound like much of an assertion to say that we of the Reverend X generation are, by and large, taking to heart the notion that our congregations must once again hold as central to their identity the fact that they are a spiritual community first and foremost. However, I think that it is precisely by paying too much attention to so many competing agendas and demands and issues of the day that we have found ourselves off track and out of sync with those seeking a church community now. Think of all the jokes suggesting that we don't know who we are, and of all of the comments many of us have heard from family members and others who insist that Unitarian Universalism is not a religion. How has it come to this? We've allowed it to be thus. We have smiled or laughed or played along with the diminishment of our faith. As important as a sense of humor is and as much as we don't want to be seen as harboring an inflated sense of self-regard, it has gone way too far. It has gotten to the point that, I believe, some among us have bought into this whole line of thinking. I hear it in newcomer sessions when someone who has been a UU in the past and is now returning says that one of the things they most appreciate about our tradition is the fact that you can believe whatever you want. I cringe when I hear this. We have accepted the false notion that there is no substance to our faith—no ultimacy (sense of the Divine or something greater than what my ego thinks or believes), nothing that holds us together (we all happen to show up at the same building every Sunday, but we all believe as we please and mostly not alike). Why have we become so complicit in the charge that there is no "there" in Unitarian Universalism? Why don't we speak up for ourselves?

Members of the Reverend X generation are doing just that. We are saying unabashedly and clearly that being a faith matters, and that in honoring the tradition in which we stand we need to define for ourselves and others who we are. Saying that our faith matters means being willing to embrace our faith tradition as a spiritual path. It means being open to leadership and vision that draws us out of complacency and convenience.

Spiritual substance comes first. What we believe and the implications of who that calls us to be in the world are integral and critical to our survival as a movement. We are a faith tradition that knocks on your door and knows precisely why. We are knocking because the world is in urgent need of our message, which says that all people matter (and even more shockingly, are worthy of God's love). The planet cries out for better stewardship, and our theology beckons us to see that the well-being of our earth is intrinsically linked with our own future; that peoples in other parts of the globe cry out for peace and we must hear and heed their cry; that people in our towns and cities cry out for food and shelter and a way of life that values being over doing—a way that knows all souls are worthy of love. Although we are younger than some, we are old enough not to be naïve about what it will take to make this shift. What I am suggesting is a significant cultural change for many in our midst, and we have much to do in introducing ourselves to new people. This is certainly more than enough to be a life's work in ministry— work we feel called to. A ministry worth sharing has been given to us to carry forth from a rich tradition that asks nothing less of us. We stand in a long line of visionary thinkers and believers who call to us. What they dreamed is ours to do, indeed!

OUR QUESTION-MARK FAITH

JENNIFER CROW

The year was 1961. Robert Frost read poetry at John F. Kennedy's inauguration, the Cold War escalated, and the Peace Corps was formed. Hope and tension, possibility and fear pervaded the country. After generations of speculation and negotiation, the Unitarians and the Universalists came together to consolidate their movements and to elect the new president of their association, Dana McLean Greely. Amid all of this, tucked away in a small city in upstate New York, a growing Unitarian church commissioned a nationally known architect to design its new building.

The architect, Louis Kahn, listened carefully to the minister and the congregation as they described the nature of Unitarian Universalism and of their church, and their hopes to create a building that reflected the essence of their faith community. Facing the initial congregational meeting, Kahn turned to an empty blackboard and began to draw. The design of the new building took shape first with the worship space, then with corridors framing the sanctuary, and finally with classrooms encircling the whole. And there, at the center of it all, stood a question mark.

For Kahn, the question mark clearly represented "the form expression of the church." The question mark emerged as Kahn's "first reaction to what may be a direction in the building of a Unitarian Church." Having heard the minister express a sense of Unitarian aspirations, Kahn said, "It occurred to me that the sanctuary is merely the center of questions." The walkway that encircled the sanctuary expressed yet another important aspect of the church community. In describing this walkway, Kahn recalled, "I drew the ambulatory to respect the fact that what is being said or what is felt in the sanctuary [is] not necessarily something you have to participate in."

In listening and responding to the congregation's self-understanding and hopes for the future, the insightful architect had captured two defining characteristics of this singular congregation and of our merging faith at that unique point in time. Through his initial drawings for a new Unitarian church building in 1961, Louis Kahn masterfully mirrored for us our lack of clarity concerning our basic, binding beliefs, as well as our entrenched reluctance to encourage active participation and membership in our church communities. As we move into the 21st century nearly 50 years later, these two challenges haunt us still, and the time is right to address them both.

Current Church Context

In the mid-20th century, as Unitarians and Universalists came together to form a new movement, churches of various denominations all over the country began to take on a new role in society. With the autonomous individual asserting pride of place as the ultimate authority in answering questions of how to live, the church had been removed from its place in society as the custodian of national morality and ethics, explains Diana Butler Bass in *The Practicing Congregation* (24). "Many mainstream congregations," Bass goes on to tell us in *Christianity for the Rest of Us*, "became a kind of Christian version of the Rotary Club, understanding the church as a religious place for social acceptability and business connections. . . . Everyone was welcome—with no spiritual demands other than to conform to some sort of generalized Protestant morality" (36).

With the church serving more as social club than as moral and spiritual guide, membership demands declined, and in time, so did church numbers. Sociologist Dean Kelley verified this trend in 1972 with the publication of his book *Why Conservative Churches Are Growing*. In that book Kelley asserted that churches that made demands on their members grew, while mainstream churches that made no demands on their members declined. Over time, Kelley's thesis has been confirmed, and in our own day and age we must come to accept the fact that religiously demanding churches are growing churches.

In a culture that over the past 50 years has shifted for many Americans from one to two earners per household, from co-parenting to single parenting, from savings to debt management, from Sundays off to Sundays on the run, this correlation of higher membership demands and church growth may not make much sense on first glance. If we look deeper, however, to the sense of fragmentation that many Americans are experiencing in this fast-paced, consumer-driven culture, perhaps it is not so surprising that Americans are searching for and embracing faith communities that help them to make sense of their worlds and to live more authentic lives. In his recent book *The Almost Church*, church consultant Michael Durall reflected on the questions that bring people to church. He found that these leading-edge questions now are: How can I lead a deeper spiritual life? How can I be engaged with something beyond day-to-day secular life? How can I be part of a community of meaning and purpose?

In contemporary society, where nomadic spirituality has been a given for many for most of their lives, a shift in American religion is occurring (*Christianity for the Rest of Us*, 23). This shift, described by Princeton sociologist Robert Wuthnow in *After Heaven*, written in the late 1990s, can best be described as a shift from seeker spirituality to practice-oriented spirituality (168). On the whole, individuals who make their way to our churches are no longer interested in walking the hallways around our sanctuaries, considering whether they'd like to join in. Individuals who make their way to our churches today come longing to jump in with both feet, hoping and expecting to find in our congregations not only questions at the center of their newfound faith but also tools that can help them to answer those questions. In this age of secularism and fragmentation, I believe, along with Diana Butler Bass, that the real vocation of our congregations is to turn tourists into pilgrims (*The Practicing Congregation*, 60).

Turning tourists into pilgrims is the task at hand, not only as we welcome new people into Unitarian Universalism but also as we invite our current members to deepen their experience of, and their commitment to, our faith. This journey will call upon us to do two things. First, we must answer the questions at the center of our faith for ourselves, experiencing firsthand the transformation that occurs when we can both articulate and live into our beliefs. Second, we must invite the tourists to come in out of the hallways, offering a pilgrimage of substance and depth that can help heal the fragmentation of our modern world, creating through our churches the beloved community of love and justice we so long for in this world.

In this unique place and time, we are lucky to be lifted up in our journey by the tide of our current culture and by the reports recently offered within our association. In a broader culture, where the locus of moral authority has shifted from the church to the individual and the individual longs to go on a journey that combines a deeper understanding of tradition with an emphasis on integrating personal spiritual experience, Unitarian

Universalism—with its long-held belief in the importance of individual conscience, reason, and experience in matters of faith—is uniquely poised to reach out and serve the needs of ever more individuals. The recent work of our past two Commissions on Appraisal will serve us well as we move forward, too. Their reports on membership and theology point the way and offer clear suggestions of how Unitarian Universalism might move forward, growing in depth and in numbers in this new day and age.

ONE SOLUTION

The most recent Commission on Appraisal report, *Engaging Our Theological Diversity*, released in 2005, made this suggestion: Perhaps it would be beneficial, the commission wrote, if UUs had their own distinctively UU spiritual path, something we could use to explore our own depths and increase our depth of spiritual exploration, without having to go outside the UU faith (90). We know, as Professor David Bumbaugh of Meadville Lombard Theological School writes in the report, that if we are truly to ground and transform our faith, "It will not be enough to offer people the opportunity to 'build your own theology.' They must be offered the freedom to build their own theology in the context of a community which is asking serious and probing religious questions, and has the courage to make deep and profound affirmations—questions and affirmations rooted in a sense of who we are and what we are profoundly about" (81).

I couldn't agree more, and for the last three years I've been hard at work with members of my congregation creating a program of Unitarian Universalist spiritual deepening that draws on our own unique history and traditions to guide us in forming a faith that works today. This program, called "Wellspring," takes a small group of committed Unitarian Universalists on a ten-month journey through our history and theology while emphasizing and supporting the adoption of a daily spiritual practice and work with a spiritual director. The intentional integration of Unitarian Universalist spiritual practices—practices like meditation, writing, listening, prayer, and memorization of poetry and sacred texts, just to name a few—combined with monthly individual spiritual direction and an ongoing small-group experience, offers something new to our efforts to write and live into our own stories of Unitarian Universalist transformation.

For years Unitarian Universalists have looked outside their churches for spiritual deepening, mistakenly assuming that our modern-day tradition offers nothing beyond pleasant interfaith gatherings designed to offend no one. The good news as we answer the call of our congregations and of the Commissions on Appraisal, is clear. Unitarian Universalism has much to offer to us and to our world. Its rich Universalist heritage of faith, hope, and love and its Unitarian legacy of freedom, reason, and tolerance combine to build a powerful foundation and a life-giving, life-transforming faith for today.

As we answer the call to reinvent ourselves and to develop a church and a theology that can assist us in facing the fragmentation and evil present in our world today, the good news is that we have a tradition that can help us do just that. The good news is that we have what we need, if only we will take a look back and do as our very own prophet, Ralph Waldo Emerson, asked: breathe new life into old traditions. We share in a long line of religious history that values innovation, that welcomes the ongoing revelation of the Holy, that calls us to forge our beliefs in the fire of our own conscience and experience. The good news of our journey is that here, in our own faith community, we can find what we need.

Throughout the Wellspring program, participants move through an exploration of Unitarian and Universalist history—learning about everything from our Unitarian roots in Transylvania to our place in the civil rights movement here in the United States. Participants study theology together, gaining a working understanding of process theology, humanism, and transcendentalism. They explore theologies of evil, crisis, and joy, while constantly seeking to understand how these theologies take shape in their own lives. They challenge and support one another while also engaging in an individual daily spiritual practice, and together they grow in their ability to articulate what it is that they believe—and what those beliefs call them to do and to be in the world. One recent Wellspring graduate heard the call to the ministry during her year of participation and has enrolled in seminary and started a Web log—*www.uuwellspring.org*—to share the Wellspring curriculum and study guide and to offer inspiration to others.

It is no coincidence that nearly half of the participants in the Wellspring program at the First Unitarian Church of Rochester this past year are new-comers to Unitarian Universalism, hoping to be transformed from tourists into pilgrims. It is no surprise that two of last year's participants are now serving as Wellspring facilitators themselves, and it is no surprise that our current board president is a Wellspring graduate and that two of our most recent nominees to the board are Wellspring members. Our lay leader of small-group ministry is a Wellspring alumna, and I can only imagine what next year's participants will choose to do. The Wellspring program offers a deep historical, theological, and spiritual grounding for its participants—and from this grounding springs a desire to put faith into action through service.

Throughout the Wellspring program, participants develop a practice of reverence through their own daily spiritual practice, and they support one another as they live into their beliefs through practical service. A typical Wellspring meeting, held on the average every two weeks, consists of a maximum of eight participants and one facilitator. The participants and the facilitator sign on for the entire ten-month program, and absences are kept to a minimum. Meetings open with the lighting of the chalice, the reading of a relevant piece of poetry, a brief silent meditation, and a time to check in about how one's spiritual practice and spiritual direction are going. From there, the group moves into a discussion of the readings, with topics ranging from "Unitarian Universalism and the Crises of Life" to "American Universalism" or "Science and Religion." All meetings close with discussion of the question "So what?" as participants are asked to articulate what relevance this new information may have to their lives. They then share words of gratitude for their time together and extinguish the chalice. While the Wellspring program cannot cover everything, it does offer a clear response to the Commission on Appraisal's suggestion that we need not only a language of reverence but a practice of reverence as well.

I have been happily surprised to find that leading a Wellspring group has done wonders for my own spiritual practice and sense of commitment to our faith. Leading a Wellspring group not only calls the facilitator to re-engage with Unitarian Universalist history and theology in a congregational setting; it also reinforces the leader's own commitment and accountability to his or her spiritual life. Despite the time commitment required, I found leading Wellspring as a facilitator—and now as a facilitator of the facilitators—inspiring, renewing, and grounding.[1]

The time is right. The moment is now—to claim our history, to strengthen our foundation, to develop the habit of daily spiritual practice grounded in the Unitarian Universalist tradition, to proclaim transformation as the guiding purpose of our churches. Whether your congregation adopts Wellspring or some other program of Unitarian Universalist spiritual deepening matters little. What matters most is that somehow we find a way to reach back into the depths of our tradition together, forming ourselves anew as individuals and as churches. The time is right, and the moment is now—to move forward with new life and new confidence, ushering in an era of renewed relevance and strength for this faith we love.

Moving Forward

This unique moment in time brings together two emerging movements in American religion. One is the shift from seeker spirituality to practice-oriented spirituality; the other is the move toward the individual as the locus of moral authority. Both of these trends have created fertile ground for Unitarian Universalism in America. "The upside of individual autonomy," Diana Butler Bass writes in *The Practicing Congregation*, "is that people must take spiritual, moral, and ethical responsibility for themselves, thus giving them a higher stake in their choices. When they join congregations or religious movements, they do so because they believe in them and find something congruent with their life experience in a particular gathering. In short, they are potentially more committed churchgoers when they walk in the door of a church than their parents, who (perhaps) remained faithful out of communal loyalty rather than personal choice" (26-7). These individuals join us, longing to make the move from tourists to pilgrims, eager to commit to a spiritual way of life that offers the promise of a deep-rooted tradition and the practical tools that they will need to answer their guiding questions. Mainline churches in America have been changing, Bass asserts, and the ones that are thriving have become practicing congregations. Practicing congregations, she tells us, appear to be succeeding in this current environment by heightening a sense of religious consciousness while also cultivating a more demanding sense of membership in the congregation by adapting tradition through meaningful practices (52).

In this unique place and time, we are lucky to be lifted up in our journey by the tide of our current culture and by the directions currently called for within our association. Both of our most recent Commissions on Appraisal have asked us to offer deeper paths to congregational membership that help Unitarian Universalists develop a sense of identity and calling. Our leadership has called us to engage in this work at this time not only for our own edification, but also because it is clear that with our current growth rate—of approximately one new member per congregation per year—we will not thrive unless we can clearly articulate what we believe and exactly what those beliefs call us to do and be in the world. If we continue to offer question-mark theology and ask little of our members, Unitarian Universalism will, in time, wither and die. It is up to us to offer something different, something deeper and, dare I say, something even more challenging to our congregations.

We have survived our merger and continue to get our feet underneath us organizationally. It is time now to deepen our understandings and our commitments. It is time to move beyond the question mark as our guiding theological symbol. As we grow in our ability to speak openly and honestly about our experiences and our beliefs, we will grow in strength as individuals and as a movement. We will move beyond the embarrassment and discomfort that so many of us experience when we are called to speak about our faith to others. We will move beyond an apologetic description of our faith that tells people what we don't believe to a faith of strength and clarity that tells people what we do believe. In this way I agree with Michael Durall: "To create an authentic church will require a conviction in our hearts and minds that Unitarian Universalism can change people's lives for the better in some fundamental way" (11). Intentional programs of Unitarian Universalist Spiritual Deepening can offer this forum for transformation.

After all, "Transformation is the fundamental purpose of and reason for a religion of seriousness and depth," Durall notes, and we will have to grow deeper if we are to transform ourselves as individuals and as congregations (103). Growing in strength and vitality requires that we change the way we view church, shifting, as Durall suggested, so that we understand church "not as a place for accumulating information but as a process of forming a people." Change is possible for us "if the church engages not the intellect alone, but the whole person; and instead of reflecting the consumer society, churches provide members an alternative way of life" (18). Cultivating this alternative way of life, this experience of transformation for ourselves and for our world, is in fact our reason for being as a church community, and it is up to us to continue developing new ways to encourage transformation within our churches.

Meaningful Membership

Looking back on those architectural drawings of a growing Unitarian church in Rochester, New York, in 1961, what does it tell us that an insightful architect declared that the form expression of our faith was a question mark, and how does this shared history call us to respond? The question-mark faith of our past tells us that the next generations have work to do. We have work to do in defining the theologies that will lead us forward, encouraging us to wrestle with the questions at the center of our being and emerging with a faith that can sustain us as we go about creating a more just and compassionate community on this earth. We have work to do as we continue our heritage of respecting difference and encouraging, as Thoreau urged, the constant search for sunlight shining in on our souls. We have work to do as we come to believe in ourselves and in the answers we find, that we might invite those folk walking our hallways to come in, and to be transformed by what they find not only in our churches but in their own hearts and minds as well.

We must, however, significantly alter our expectations of church membership if we are to capture the moment and serve the needs of those in our churches and of those coming our way. No longer will we build churches framed by the expectation that "what is being said or what is felt in the sanctuary [is] not necessarily something you have to participate in," as Jean France writes on the First Unitarian Church of Rochester's website when describing Kahn's vision for the new church building in 1961. Our desire to offend no one, to require next to nothing of our members, to welcome diversity of belief as a goal overriding authenticity and clarity, has held us back as a community of faith. A deeper and broader understanding of the meaning of membership, as the Commission on Appraisal reported in 2001, "is vital to our growth. The individual personal spiritual growth of each person who identifies with Unitarian Universalism and the growth of our congregations depend on deepening the theological understandings of membership" (103). In addition to strengthening our requests of church members for increased financial and leadership support, I believe that it is time that we take up the charge offered by both of the most recent Commissions on Appraisal, inviting members new and old to wrestle actively with questions of theology and spiritual practice as an expectation of their membership in our churches.

Note

1. Starting a Wellspring program at your congregation couldn't be easier right now. Thanks largely to the dedication of two lay leaders, Libby Moore and Joy Collins, a curriculum, complete with reading suggestions and a week-by-week class outline is available at no cost on our website, *www.uuwellspring.org*.

Works Cited

Bass, Diana Butler. *Christianity for the Rest of Us: How the Neighborhood Church Is Transforming the Faith.* San Francisco: Harper San Francisco, 2006.

————. *The Practicing Congregation: Imagining a New Old Church.* Herndon, Va.: Alban Institute, 2004.

Durall, Michael. *The Almost Church: Redefining Unitarian Universalism for a New Era.* Tulsa: Jenkin Lloyd Jones Press, 2004.

France, Jean. *http://www.rochesterunitarian.org/Building_desc.html*

Kelley, Dean. *Why Conservative Churches Are Growing: A Study in the Sociology of Religion.* Mercer University Press, 1972.

Unitarian Universalist Association. Commission on Appraisal. *Belonging: The Meaning of Membership.* Boston: Unitarian Universalist Association, 2001.

————. *Engaging Our Theological Diversity.* Boston: Unitarian Universalist Association, 2005.

Wuthnow, Robert. *After Heaven: Spirituality in America Since the 1950s.* Berkeley: University of California Press, 1998.

DIGGING DEEP: OUR COMMUNAL RESPONSIBILITY TO OUR PRINCIPLES

JOHN A. CULLINAN

At a recent gathering of ministers, a group discussion about the nature of congregational covenants turned toward the nature of relationships *within* a covenant—specifically the relationship between an individual and a community. Among ministers, at least, there seemed to be no lack of strong emotions tied to the idea of "the individual." Some spoke in celebration of the diverse personalities within their congregations and of the richness and depth that each brought to congregational life. Others decried the selfish individualism flowing unfettered through their communities and of the potential for unrest and destruction brought on by self-centered and self-justifying behavior. Intense feelings emerged from both sides of the discussion, yet all involved seemed to agree that the individual, by necessity, is the base unit—the building block—of a congregation. More important, all seemed to agree that, for better or for worse, this idea of the individual as building block seemed to be an implication of the Unitarian Universalist Association's First Principle, to "affirm and promote the inherent worth and dignity of each person."

In 2006, a few months earlier at General Assembly in St. Louis, William Schulz, former president of the UUA and former Executive Director of Amnesty International USA, delivered the annual Berry Street Lecture, "What Torture's Taught Me." In it, he described the process by which a seemingly reasonable man might be transformed into a modern monster, a torturer. "In what sense," Schulz asked, "can we defend the notion that a torturer is a person of '*inherent* worth and dignity'?" Later he again asked,

"Who is this creature of 'inherent dignity' who is so easily led astray?" Schulz's experiences with Amnesty International have led him to question the notion of inherent worth and dignity, to question what is meant when we say "inherent," and to challenge the notion that this idea of worth and dignity is really inherent after all.

In talking with other ministers and listening to Schulz's impassioned dialogue, I sense a deep desire among Unitarian Universalists to delve into those principles we hold so dear and to try to live them out practically in a world that seems to operate in defiance of them. It is, I believe, a primary duty of liberal religious people to dig deep into the layers of meaning within the symbols of their faith so that those symbols remain vital and practical and do not degrade into idols. In a faith based in reason and freedom, I would expect that these conversations might happen frequently. I would hope that Schulz is not the only one wrestling with the idea of inherency, and that not only clergy are debating the idea of the individual. This is my expectation.

The reality, I have found, is far different. Deep exploration is rare, and day-to-day engagement with our Principles, sadly, borders on idolatry.

X X X

Consider the following anecdotes. Years ago, while I was working as a youth advisor, an interesting chat took place on the advisors' message board: A woman had come to the director of religious education at a church looking to volunteer as a teacher. In the course of their conversation, she admitted that she made the bulk of her living as a dominatrix. The DRE was troubled by this and explained that he found himself with a dilemma. "Do I," he wondered, "ignore this information and take on a willing volunteer? Or do I reject her and avoid the potential for controversy, or worse?"

"Don't turn her down!" came one response.

"How can you reject this person?"

And finally, "Don't say no to her. It wouldn't be *affirming to her inherent worth and dignity*." This last response would become the one echoed by a large number of chat group participants.

I was astonished. Somewhere along the line a concept as open and multifaceted as "affirming inherent worth and dignity" had been recast in someone's mind as the maxim "Don't say no to people." The fact that so many responses were in sympathy with this last sentiment told me that it wasn't only a single person's misunderstanding. Somehow, within the context of that community, the Unitarian Universalist First Principle had been transformed into a tool by which the individual was absolved of the responsibility to make judgments or to be accountable to community. The maxim "Don't say no to people" had overruled the individual's reasoning capacity.

Years later, I gave a sermon about the need to engage with our Principles more deeply. I related the previous anecdote to illustrate a main point: Regardless of the *content* of our judgment, the purpose of the First Principle is not to provide us with a simplistic maxim to absolve us of our responsibilities to the larger community.

I had wanted to generate a dialogue about the Principles and how they might become tools for developing religious identity. However, some in the pews that day could not get past the fact that I had placed the idea of judgment into the conversation. People were angry.

"How could you judge her like that?" they wanted to know.

"What gives you the right?"

Rather than grasping my main point—that the maxim "Don't say no" did not do the First Principle justice—there were some who fully embraced the maxim (and, ironically, made judgments about me and my willingness to make judgments). In addition to the "Don't say no" maxim, a new simplistic maxim entered the conversation: "It's not your life, or your decision." More succinctly: "Don't judge other people"—as if to say that because of some notion of absolute personal sovereignty, the individual is exempt from accountability to his or her community.

These experiences, I will admit up front, do not translate into a diagnosis for the entire movement. However, neither are these isolated incidents or aberrations. There is a Pollyanna-hued aura around the First Principle that can lead to individual interpretations of similar weightlessness, the same sort of aura that leads Bill Schulz to question its integrity.

It was never meant to be this way. The sad fact is that all of these simplistic surface readings and all of this cockeyed optimism betray the intention of those who carved out the language of our Principles and Purposes.

x x x

The Principles and Purposes as they exist today are the result of many years of often difficult debate, learning, and deep soul-searching. It was one of the first religious statements to be intentionally gender-neutral. It was intended to speak purposefully of where the movement had come from (the five sources), where its members understood it to be then, and where they wanted it to move (the seven principles).

Walter Royal Jones, the retired minister who oversaw the primary working group of the new Principles (as referenced in Warren Ross's *The Premise and the Promise*) makes several important observations about the current wording: First, almost all of the concepts were anticipated by the earlier statement of principles from 1961 except for the seventh; second, changing "free and *disciplined* search for truth and meaning" to "free and *responsible* search for truth and meaning" was meant to indicate that the search takes place within community; finally, the word "inherent" replaced the word "supreme," indicating that "the potentiality of every person is 'capable of being hidden or rejected, even betrayed'" (Ross, 98).

Beyond these original intentions was the fact that the Principles' designers foresaw the eventual obsolescence of their hard-won wording. Warren Ross notes that "a free and responsible search for truth and meaning carries within it the seeds of its own obsolescence." Included in the language of the UUA's bylaws is a mandate to review the language of the Principles and Purposes within a 15-year period, a task taken up by the UUA's Commission on Appraisal in mid-2005.

The work of those who dedicated themselves to framing our Principles and Purposes was intended to avoid the pitfalls of shallow engagement and trivialization that crop up with such alarming regularity now. Inherency *is* transient. The individual *should* be accountable to the community. However, what was intended was not explicated. This omission is far from surprising.

Liberal religion is, historically, loathe to make explicit statements about the more negative aspects of human nature. While we know in our minds and hearts that people make bad choices and do bad things, historic liberal faith statements rarely say so. Inherency may imply transience, but what happens when worth and dignity are subsumed? Does the "arc of history bend toward justice" all by itself? Can it be bent toward injustice if enough people pull it that way? Does humanity really progress "onward and upward forever and ever"? Could it not be dragged down by its own imperfections? Humankind is equally capable of moving in both directions, and yet the historic focus of liberal religion has always been on the inevitability of the positive—usually in opposition to our more orthodox cousins' narrow focus on human depravity. All the while, history challenges us to come up with a more realistic, holistic answer.

In 1934 this challenge to account for the whole of human nature was brought directly to our doorstep. That year, the American Unitarian Association invited Reinhold Niebuhr, professor of practical theology at Union Theological Seminary in New York, to deliver the year's Ware Lecture at the Association's annual May meeting. Niebuhr himself had once been a practitioner of liberal religion and, in the early part of his career, an outright optimist regarding human nature. He had believed wholeheartedly in the tenets of the social gospel, had worked closely with union organizers in his bustling Detroit parish, and had been an active and committed member of the Socialist Party. Niebuhr, in short, believed that the progression of humanity "onward and upward forever" was an inevitable, unstoppable force within history. As late as 1930, this was still the core of his faith.

By 1934, however, when he arrived in Boston to deliver his Ware Lecture, Niebuhr was a changed man. The meteoric rise of Nazism in Germany, all of the evil that advent entailed, and the subsequent suffering and oppression of so many of his kin and colleagues had led him to abandon his optimistic outlook. Niebuhr still held on to a spark of hope; he didn't sink into a purely pessimistic view of humanity, but he came to believe that a religion that did not take into account the fullness of human nature, its potential for both good and evil, was inadequate. This is the meat of the challenge Niebuhr brought to the Unitarians' door in his lecture "Pessimistic Optimism."

"The religion of modern culture," he told those gathered that day, "is a superficial religion which has discovered a meaningful world without having discovered the perils to meaning in death, sin, and catastrophe."

For Niebuhr, the arc of history could not bend toward justice *without* the existence of injustice—and progress was not self-propelled or inevitable. "History does not move forward without catastrophe, happiness is not guaranteed by the multiplication of physical comforts, social harmony is not easily created by more intelligence, and human nature is not as good or as harmless as had been supposed."

His challenge to religious liberalism is thus summed up: "An adequate religion is always an ultimate optimism which has entertained all the facts which lead to pessimism."

Niebuhr himself could account for a sense of meaning in the entirety of human nature only within the context of what he saw as the revelation of God's salvation through Jesus. He would eventually deny outright the notion that reason alone, one of the prime sources of authority within the

Unitarian tradition, could ever adequately make meaning out of the whole of human nature.

Despite his rebuke of our faith in reason and our unwillingness to follow him toward orthodoxy, his challenge to the liberal view of human nature remains a legitimate one. The potential for both good and ill exists within each of us. Niebuhr challenged liberals for lifting up the good and downplaying the evil just as much as he challenged conservatives for touting the depravity of man while denying the possibility of inherent goodness. When he published his systematic theology in 1941, he could not allow a doctrine of original sin to exist unless it stood in tandem with a doctrine of original justification. Issues of orthodoxy aside, Niebuhr's doctrine of human nature is both pragmatic and true. It is the heart of his critique of liberal religion 75 years ago.

Have we answered the challenge?

X X X

We certainly intended to, as Walter Royal Jones's testimony illustrates. Within all of the debate and wordsmithery leading to our current Principles was the tacit acknowledgment that *yes*, human beings are capable of abrogating or burying their essential worth, and *yes*, the individual is accountable to his or her community.

What has happened in the interim?

The implications, unbolstered by explicit statements of intent, have given way to shallow dialogue and simplistic maxims. Minus the context of original intent, the language of our Principles has become open to ambiguity—an ambiguity that does not lead to sufficient discussion or exploration, or at least meaningful discussion or exploration. This ambiguity minus the discussion leads to the fabrication of shallow maxims. Each individual arrives at a self-determined definition of the terms within the Principles and carries on with the assumption that the arrived-at definition is, in fact, the standard. Thus, one person's intention to define *inherence* as including the concepts "impermanent" or "expendable" becomes another's maxim: "Don't judge others."

The ambiguity of definition minus discussion leads us to the breakdown between those who celebrate the individual and those who decry individualism—all in the name of inherent worth and dignity. Looking back to that discussion among my colleagues, I began to question whether the problem might be that we don't have a clear definition of what we mean when we say *person*. In my online community, I tried a simple exercise. "Within the context of the First Principle, define *person*," I asked my audience. Over the next week I received several answers. All were as creative and individual as the people who composed them, and while several could be lumped together in categories, no two were exactly the same. The definitions ranged from the specifically biological to the broadly esoteric: accounting for one species, or more; accounting for nature and/or nurture; accounting for spirit or soul or consciousness. Everyone knew what *person* meant to them; but *person* did not mean one thing to all people.

Looking again at the idea of inherence, even Schulz appears to assume a definition of inherency that seems more permanent than transient. Schulz, impelled by the difference he observes between the Principles as they are understood and the reality, delves deep into the meaning of the inherence. Inherency, he finally decides, "is a political construct.... Each of us has to be assigned worth."

This conclusion leads to more and better questions: "But who does the assigning of worth? How do we decide that something is a sin? How do we know that torture is wrong? What is the basis for human rights?" Schulz goes on to attempt answers to these questions, and the address has been perhaps *the* most talked about event over the past year among Unitarian Universalists.

It is, then, fortuitous timing that the UUA's Commission on Appraisal has picked up the long overdue work of revisiting the language of the Principles. As I write this, there are a little more than two years left in the Commission's process. Plenty of time to wrestle with meaning and intention. Plenty of time to deal with ambiguity and oversimplification. As the Commission continues its process, here are my hopes for what the ends might entail:

1. CONTEXT

If the Principles are a part of a covenant between congregations, they need to behave more like a classic covenant. Historic covenant models have almost always included a brief history of how a people came to need and form a covenant, a road map of "How We Got Here." The history of the Principles' composition and the memories of those who participated are out there, but not explicit in the work itself.

Where do we learn the story? For myself, I was three years and several thousands of dollars into a seminary education before I learned the story. It's not a method I'd recommend to just anyone. Outside the seminary, I've never heard the story related from the pulpit or told in a new-member orientation. The story of how all this came to be is equally as important as the end product. The story of how all this came to be would enhance the meaning of the end product. The story of how all this came to be should be part of the end product.

2. Rules of Engagement

Along with the content of the Principles and their context, a much more intentional means needs to be developed both for keeping the Principles at the forefront of congregational consciousness and for constructing frameworks for deep engagement and conversation. Once again, classical covenant formulations provide us the model, giving explicit instructions as to the methods of *deposition* of the covenant: how and where it will be read, displayed, and thus reinforced in the minds and hearts of the covenanted.

Now, display is not really a major issue. The listing of the Principles and Purposes is ubiquitous in Unitarian Universalist publications, at the front of hymnals, on posters in classrooms, on wallet cards and pamphlets for visitors. But the purpose of the classical rules of deposition was to maintain the covenant in the consciousness of the people. For a covenant whose stipulations consist of explicit "thou shalt not" directives, display and awareness are potentially sufficient for maintenance. However, for a document such as ours, in which there needs to be room for wide discussion about meaning, intent, and practice, mere awareness is not sufficient. We need more to maintain our covenant.

It is important to note here that the Principles and Purposes are part of a covenant among congregations, a fact that is often trotted out by individuals who object to the "creeping creedalism" of the Principles. That being the case, it is most certainly the responsibility of individual congregations to come to a corporate understanding of what the stipulations of this covenant mean (define, for example, "free," "responsible," or "equity"), and how they will practice them. It is this process of corporate understanding that should make up the meat of the deposition of our covenant. The community must be responsible for making meaning and practicality out of the Principles. It should be a dynamic process, constantly renewed. New members of the community, who more often than not are asked to be in sympathy with the Principles as a stipulation of membership, can then be presented with a living covenant rather than just a list; they can be asked to be in sympathy with embodied principles, and to be more ready to bring their own experience and meaning-making capacity into the communal process.

Congregations engaged in this process of maintenance thus might bring about a much more organic process of revisiting without the need for by-law mandates, commissions, or decades-long intervals of stagnation.

3. A Realistic Accounting of Human Nature

Niebuhr's challenge to the American Unitarian Association in 1934 still stands without an explicit answer. We understand at some level that evil exists in the world and that people are equally as capable of depravity as they are of dignity. We just don't say it outright. To speak explicitly of the dark side of human nature is not to damn humanity for eternity, but to open our hearts and minds to the full potential of humanity and to name that which we hope to stand against. We must name it to do so.

Recently I asked a roomful of students, after they had read Niebuhr's address, how Unitarian Universalism deals with the reality of human evil. Some refused to acknowledge the word, fearing the sense of judgment contained within it. Some spoke of good words heard here and there from ministers or others. When I asked where Unitarian Universalism dealt *explicitly* with human evil, they all agreed the answer was "Nowhere." The closest they could come to anything that approached an example was Bill Schulz's Berry Street address.

Nearly three-quarters of a century later, Schulz echoes the challenge delivered by Reinhold Niebuhr. Our outlook on human nature is still insufficient. It does not account for the dark places in the human soul. It is perhaps irresponsible to speak it in the presence of the tortured. Schulz does not stand alone in his renewal of the challenge. In defense of his own argument, he calls upon the memory of James Luther Adams, a contemporary of Niebuhr and our premier theologian, who almost a decade after Niebuhr's Ware Lecture reiterated his challenge to liberal religion in his Berry Street Essay, "The Changing Reputation of Human Nature." Schulz speaks of Adams's argument that liberal religion "has neglected these [negative] aspects of human nature in its zeal to proclaim the spark of divinity in man."

At a recent ordination I attended, the charge to the minister included a paraphrasing of Rabbi Irving Greenberg: speak no theology that does not make sense in the presence of a burning child. Again and again, the challenge to account for the whole reality of human nature has been laid at our feet from both within and without our movement. If I can have only one wish on this list granted, it is this: that we take up the challenge; that our religion may speak Principles that account for, and make sense to the victims of, human suffering. To do anything less would be, I fear, eventually to render ourselves irrelevant.

HOW THE PRINCIPLES AND PURPOSES ARE LEADING UUs ASTRAY

Marlin Lavanhar

Faith is not delivered to us in a package of words; it is a grace overwhelming.
— Wallace W. Robbins

We cannot be religious in general.
— George Santayana

n the gospels Jesus avoids self-definition by asking, "Who do *they* say I am?" In doing so, the great leader allowed others to characterize him, rather than defining himself. In his day this question led some people to think he was the Messiah, others to think he was the Son of God. Some thought of him as a political threat, and others considered him a loose cannon. In a similar way, the Unitarian Universalist Association's (UUA's) Principles are characterized by various people in a variety of disparate ways. Depending on one's relationship to the Principles, they are glorified by some as almost salvific, while at the same time they are derided by others as a troubling nuisance best dealt with through extermination. Different people define the Principles as being essentially an article of bylaws, a covenant, a creed, a mission or vision statement, scripture, a theology, the permanent (as opposed to the transient) summation of Unitarian Universalist faith, and as the minimum that binds Unitarian Universalists (UUs) together. This lack of consistent definition of the roles and purposes of the Principles has led to their wide misuse in ways that are having a significantly negative impact on UU identity, theology, and congregational life.

According to the Commission on Appraisal's report "Engaging Our Theological Diversity," the Principles and Purposes Statement was created with the intention of being an article of the UUA bylaws that was extremely general so as to not exclude anyone. In other words, its formation was an exercise in creative reductionism to provide a statement of the least common denominators that connect Unitarian Universalists. According to the Commission on Appraisal (COA) Report:

> In practice the Principles have emerged as a symbol of unity. The irony is that they were intended primarily as a statement of *broad inclusiveness*; that is, of a wide and even all-embracing diversity appropriate to the bylaws of a religiously heterodox movement but theologically neutral to the greatest extent possible. . . . In the words of the Committee chair, Walter Royal Jones Jr., 'We really wanted to assure everyone that no point of view was going to be left out. We wanted to say to everyone, 'You belong'" ("Engaging," 139).

As an affirmation of the least that UUs hold in common, across the theological and philosophical spectrum, the Principles do a fair, if rather uninspiring, job. However, as the Statement has morphed into being used as a defining set of principles for individuals and congregations, it has overreached its purpose and has become widely misused and misunderstood. The misunderstanding and misuse of the Statement have contributed to an identity crisis within UUism and a lack of theological depth in many congregations. Another result has been a decreasing impact of UUism on shaping the direction of liberal religion in North America.

As the Statement has drifted away from its prescribed definition and purpose over the past several decades, so in many ways has the collective UU movement. The core of the Unitarian Universalist movement has become so elusive in recent years that many, including some UU clergy, have started to refer to the center of the faith as a "doughnut hole." In other words, these UU leaders are not sure the UU tradition has a core that binds its people together.

Prior to the 1985 vote that established the Principles Statement, the Rev. Carl Scovel wrote: ". . . It is the refusal to take theology seriously which lies at the heart of our current malaise and decline" (Scovel, 128). He went on to suggest that ". . . when someone claims to be 'inclusive' and 'creedless' they are simply refusing to acknowledge their theological position, a position which necessarily includes some and excludes others" (Scovel, 130-131).

The point is not that UUs need to become creedal and exclusive. The point is that for UUism to be pluralistic as well as to offer theological depth and spiritual sustenance requires a clear distinction between: (1) the statement that speaks to the minimum that binds all UUs together, and (2) the credos, theologies, and covenants that are at the center of the practices and beliefs of individuals and congregations. Unfortunately, the distinction has become blurred.

THE FORMATION OF THE PRINCIPLES

To understand the dilemma described above, it is important to realize how the Principles were developed. They were born out of a cumbersome and questionable democratic process. Even today, the question remains whether the process used within the UUA to make governing and other decisions at a national level is an effective or even democratic way of making decisions. An even bigger question for the purposes of this chapter is whether the same process is an effective way to determine the core principles of a religious community.

The General Assembly process that is used by the UUA to make governing and other decisions on behalf of the Association has been, and remains, a significantly flawed form of representational democracy. Hundreds of member congregations do not send delegates to the GA; and among the congregations that do send delegates, the process by which their delegates are elected is typically not very representational. As one seasoned minister put it:

> . . . in most congregations most of the time, "election" of these "delegates" is strictly *pro forma*. Most members either don't know about or don't care about these "delegate" elections; so we just rubber stamp as our "choice" whoever happens to have the time or interest or money to go. And this is how we have got, in practice, a phony democracy (6 Wesley, 9).

Regarding the discussion process in the congregations that led up to the determination of the Principles, it has been equated by the Rev. Davidson Loehr with the taking of a political poll.

> . . . instead of asking religious questions about what was worth believing, what was necessary to believe, what beliefs might best be used to fashion people of good character, and so on—instead of this, the Unitarians [sic] simply took an extended poll. They asked a handful of churches— including the first church I served—to hold discussion groups, to discover what the people who attended there (and liked discussion groups) happened to believe. What such a poll had to, and did, reveal

were the generic cultural beliefs these people brought into church with them: the profile of social and political liberals (Loehr).

Keep in mind that politicians who base their positions on what the latest polls say are typically ridiculed for their lack of moral leadership. How much more ridiculous is an entire religious tradition that uses the equivalent of a poll to determine its core values?

In fairness, one has to keep in mind that the original purpose of the Statement, according to its architects, was to create a declaration for the Association's bylaws. If the Statement were merely an article of bylaws, the process would not seem as outrageous as it does now that the Statement is being used in so many significant ways.

In sum, in the early 1980s, a flawed democratic process led to what was considered a nearly all-inclusive statement, for the purpose of making as many congregations and individuals as possible feel that they could belong to the Association. Unfortunately, that statement has since come to take on a scriptural quality for some, for others a creedal quality, for others a covenantal quality, for others a theological quality—and for others it is considered an apt description of the core tenets of their personal faith and corporate religion.

USES AND MISUSES

The exceptional popularity of the Principles as a guiding statement of common commitment among individual Unitarian Universalists has been surprising. The committee members who steered the process leading to near-unanimous adoption of the Principles and Purposes never anticipated the various uses to which their work would be put ("Engaging," 126).

Opposite is a chart of notable ways in which the Principles have been used along with some correlated ways in which they have been misused since 1985.

USES	MISUSES
UUA Bylaw Statement	UU Scripture
Has helped shift the UU emphasis on individual beliefs toward statements of corporate values & commitments	Misused by individuals as their personal credo or statement of belief
A Statement of Common Agreement Among UUs Nationally (The Least Common Denominator)	Misused as a definitive statement of UU faith by churches and individuals
Unifying	Creedal
Affirms Religious Pluralism	Reflects an implicit humanist consensus
Degenderized the UU Principles	Removed God
A beginning for UU faith & Theology	Misused when seen as a UU theology or as an end in themselves
Used by churches as a responsive reading or a new member reading	Misused when they replace a congregation's discernment of its own covenant & corporate commitments
Used as a call for evangelism (It says: "We... promote...")	Misused as a tool for evangelism (vague, general, unmemorable)
Can fit on a wallet card	Misused in place of offering a personal description of one's faith
References for sermons	Doctrinaire, seen as authoritative
Used as a UU reference point in Religious Education	Misused as a limiting factor in RE curriculum development

Researching ways the Principles are used, the COA discovered:

> The Principles are frequently recited in worship and often printed on orders of worship and in newsletters; they are adapted in the place of individual Congregational covenants and prominently displayed in the front of the UU hymnal. . . . The results of all our Commission on Appraisal worship survey clearly demonstrate that the Principles and Purposes have become a common expression of UU shared faith. One of the questions asked of each congregation was, 'What written statement of purpose or description of your congregation regularly appears on your order of service or other communications?' Even though the question explicitly refers to a statement specific to the congregation, 56 of the 370 responding congregations reported that the UUA's Principles...serve that function for them. Another 86 regularly use the Principles in addition to a statement specific to the congregation ("Engaging," 126–127).

Many UU congregations have come to use the Principles as their congregation's description or statement of purpose. Goethe said, "a tradition cannot be inherited, it must be earned." By using the UUA's Principles in place of developing a congregational covenant or statement of purpose, these congregations have most likely failed to engage in the formative work that allows a community to understand itself in its place and time and in relation to its particular history. It is conceivable that a congregation could go through a process of discernment that could end in the discovery that the Principles are the best description of its particular identity and purpose as a community of faith. However, I find it improbable that this is how many of the congregations that use the Principles in this way came to use them. It is more likely that the UUA's Principles have been adopted by congregations as an easy substitute for doing the formative work of developing a covenant or theological identity or mission that is specific to them. In that way, a bylaw provision conceived through compromise and concession, intended to be a broad description of the minimum that binds UUs together, has come to shape and define the religious identity of many UU congregations and their members.

Even though "a tradition must be earned," it can also be passed down and does not need to be recreated in every generation. Judaism offers a powerful precedent for how a community bound together by a covenant can welcome new generations and individuals into the covenant. The Jewish covenant was presumably formed among those who were present at Mount Sinai when Moses returned with the commandments. Jews have developed a tradition of holy days, songs, scriptures, rituals and study that serve to initiate new generations into the covenant. Passover and other holidays recount how the Jewish people were formed as a religious body, and in effect these rituals serve to initiate new members into the covenant. The covenant and identity of UU congregations would be greatly enhanced through some process that brings new members and new generations "to the mountain" so that they can have the experience of entering the covenant of their community. A recitation of the UUA Principles is not sufficient for the task.

In a way similar to congregations, many individual UUs have come to adopt the UUA's Principles as their own credo, theology, or scripture. But the Principles are not a theology or credo or scripture. In fact, the creators stated that they worked hard to ensure that the Statement was "theologically neutral to the greatest extent possible . . ." It is important that UU leaders begin to clarify regularly for their members the purpose, formation, and limitations of the Principles. Otherwise, members who come to UU congregations are being led astray in their religious lives and identities in some fundamental ways. Surely many new members and visitors are handed the Statement and are told that these are the core principles of the UU faith.

Seeds Versus Harvest

The UUA Principles are more like seeds to be planted and tended than fruits to be harvested. Like seeds, they hold within them the promise of something larger, but they require nurture and cultivation to achieve their promise.

The Principles find fertile soil in congregations where the ideals and values expressed in the Principles are not worshiped in themselves but are explored and expanded through education, free discussion, theological understanding, historical perspective, worship, and action. One typically finds deep roots and growing branches in congregations where there is a corporate sense of calling and mission and purpose and an identity that transcends the Principles Statement of the Association. Congregations that are held together by an authentic sense of covenant contain the kind of mutual promise among people that keeps a community growing together through fair and foul weather. Fertile soil is also found in congregations where members are generous both personally and financially and therefore offer the kind of support and resources necessary for the healthy growth and expansion of the values that are only nascent and minimally expressed in the Principles themselves.

General and Particular in Religion

One frustrated young participant in the COA review of the Principles at the 2007 GA said, "I don't think, like most of you, that the Principles are the world's longest and least memorable mission statement; I consider them the world's shortest and most unforgettable scripture. As a lifelong Unitarian Universalist, they are my scripture," he exclaimed. One wonders how many UUs revere and venerate the Principles as scriptural for them. In fact, the Principles lack the essential qualities of scripture.

One major problem with generalized principle statements, like the UUA Principles, is that they lack the power and depth of life's particularities. No alcoholic, no person on her deathbed or person in need of forgiveness, no grieving parent or child, no person contemplating divorce, suicide, abortion or military service, turns to the Principles in time of need or temptation or discernment. They are not enough to sustain faith. Faith and meaning are often mediated by metaphors and stories and symbols. While the Principles may articulate what in general holds UUs together in association, the true sustaining power of faith is in the particularities of the theologies, practices, traditions, and scriptures that inform people's faith.

There is much diversity regarding which scriptures, traditions, and theologies inform different UUs and their congregations. This level of religious pluralism within one community of faith is a unique characteristic of UUism. Yet, both in the USA and the UUA, there has long been disagreement over whether it is a possibility to create a melting pot in which particular identities are meshed and melded into a coagulated whole, or whether diversity needs to be more like a salad bowl in which distinctions and particularities are maintained and celebrated. One colleague wrote:

> [I do not] suggest that we find a least common denominator among the [various theological] views, as if a diversity of religious philosophies were somehow regrettable. Each of the [theological] views singly is superior to a pale gruel made of parts of all [of them]. Because each one is at least definite about something, the result of human choice rather than an intellectual blender (Shaw, 134).

The Principles are by design a "gruel" made through boiling down the rich particularities of faiths and theologies into a common statement.

> . . . If we are to continue to retain under one umbrella . . . the broad categories of faith that now exist in the UUA, we shall all have to develop a tolerance that recognizes the PLURALISM of faiths among us and that takes the PARTICULARITIES of the faiths seriously (Hoehler, 125).

One reason often cited to explain why Christianity became so effective in co-opting and replacing many pagan religions is that it is more intuitive for people to relate to human narratives like the stories of Jesus and Mary and Joseph than it is to relate to a sacred bull or a holy rock or other abstract deities, icons, or totems. Once the metaphors of religion took names like Peter (instead of an actual rock) and John and Joseph, and these metaphors were described as walking and talking and struggling like the rest of humanity, they developed into a religion that had a powerful appeal. Christianity caught on and spread in part because of its natural correlation to real embodied human experience.

In the practice of UUism today, it seems that scripture has become increasingly marginal and has been replaced by a set of words and phrases (the Principles) that have become more and more central. To the degree that this is true, UUs have divorced their religion from a set of common stories that acknowledge the raw, breathing, blistering, bleeding, stinking aspects of human reality. In my experience, when I am weeping for my dead daughter, the image of a soiled Mary on her knees holding her son's lifeless and bloody torso against her body touches the core of my experience; the words "justice and compassion for all people . . ." are about as inspiring and comforting as a phone book.

Without a doubt, UUs still connect with the meaning-making power of narrative through the telling and retelling of the stories of certain UU martyrs. People are moved by the image of Servetus burning along with his books while tied to a stake surrounded by green wood, so that it would burn slowly and torturously to give him a chance to recant before he died. UUs can imagine Francis David in a dark and dampened dungeon using the last of his energies carving the words "neither the sword of Popes, nor the cross, nor the image of death—nothing will halt the march of truth . . ." in the wall of his cell. People relate viscerally to the image of James Reeb with his life bleeding out of him onto the pavement in the dark of night in a strange town while following his conscience to Selma, Alabama. The stories of our heroes and martyrs are stirring, and yet we also need our canon to include the stories of our Peters, the ones who wrestled with their souls and decided to deny the request to go to Selma even though they knew they could and believed they should. Our canon needs also to include other parts of these stories, as when James Reeb's wife, Marie, struggled, for months or years, with her "what ifs." For the rest of us who live lives that fall short of martyrdom and who contend with shame, fear, compromises, regrets, betrayal, temptation, and self-doubt, there need to be stories of human frailty, sin, and redemption, to accompany the stories of human heroism.

One might argue that UUs should compile a unique set of UU stories that contain the full cache of life's struggles; but then again, we already have ancient scriptures that contain a prodigious wealth of stories and metaphors, if only we are willing to read our lives through them or read them into our lives. Established scriptures, like the Bible, provide a language and set of symbols and stories shared by people around the world and throughout the centuries. These are the stories and symbols that shape communities and nations, heal wounds, restore hope, and inspire sacrifice and forgiveness. No set of general principles can offer this kind of transforming religious power.

THE SOURCES

The discussion of the particularities of faith leads naturally into an examination of the Sources section of the Statement. For the most part I appreciate the idea that the contemporary UU tradition draws from many sources for insight and wisdom. However, I am concerned that, by appearing to give equal weight to all of these sources, the Statement misrepresents the UU heritage and traditions. UUism combines two religious traditions that are primarily and historically rooted in western biblical and intellectual ideas, history, and interpretation. The linguistic, social, ethical, philosophical, and other aspects of what has become the UU tradition owe much more to western biblical and intellectual sources than they do to any of the other sources UUism claims. The failure of UUs to acknowledge this dominant foundation of UU identity and culture has significant negative consequences.

It is critical that we as an Association become more honest about our core historic identity and rootedness in the western biblical and intellectual traditions, so that we can clarify that while we draw on other sources, we do so as a people within the framework of a religious community rooted in a liberal western intellectual and Protestant heritage.

In academia today many historians and theologians introduce themselves in their writing and make it known to readers that they are writing from a particular social location. Such an introduction acknowledges that their social location and their historic and cultural context have an influence on how they understand their subject. In the same way, UUs (as a community of faith) draw on many sources, but we do so through the lens of a particular tradition.

The weight of biblical influence (religiously, intellectually, historically, and culturally) on the UU tradition and its practices and on the collective UU worldview is heavier than any of the other sources. The general failure of UUs to be honest about the (past and present) influence of Christianity and the Bible on the UU tradition is a self-deception that hinders UUs' understanding of themselves, their theologies, and their own social location. The UU movement's current dissonance about its biblical rootedness is analogous to a white, heterosexual, Anglo-Saxon, Protestant, male, American adult's denying that his social location has any influence whatsoever on his worldview, faith, and ethics. Such a denial of the roots of UUism comes in part from a position of unacknowledged privilege as well as sometimes from a desire to be something that we are not.

Some North Americans with European ancestry try to claim, for various reasons (such as guilt, insecurity and shame) and in various ways, that the fullness of their soul is betrayed by the current state of their physical incarnation. These are people who say such things as, "I was Native American in a past life." These people are forming an identity based on a denial of their true history and are posing as who they want to be instead of owning who they are. The broad denial of UUism's rootedness in western biblical traditions has a similar effect on UUism and contributes to the UU movement's recent inability to articulate a core purpose and identity as a community of faith.

Accepting that UUism is a tradition that is principally rooted in, and continues to grow out of, a western biblical and intellectual heritage does not require a denial of the rich and varied sources from which we also draw nourishment. However, such an acknowledgement sets UUism honestly in the fertile soil from which it grows and has grown. Like a plant that is nourished not only by soil but also by sun and rain and dew, UUs grow in breadth and depth from many sources of sustenance, but UUs do so planted firmly in the fertile soil of a long biblical heritage. To deny the sustaining and shaping influences of the varied sources of UU faith today would be like a plant denying the many sources of its nourishment. However, allowing ourselves to lose our self-understanding and primary identity within the western biblical tradition is equivalent to a plant's being uprooted from its soil. James Luther Adams wrote:

> We need to strike a route into a definite plot of soil. We need somehow to find our place in a continuing and promising tradition with its sacred books, its communion of saints and its disciples. We need the church's community of memory and hope through the sharing of which we may

in the fullness of time first sense our need for conversion and then grow in grace and knowledge. . . . In the church we accept the truth: *by their fruits shall you know them.* But we also accept the truth: *by their roots shall you know them.* Where there are no roots, there will be no fruit (Beach, 250).

In affirming the Source Statement, UUs have implied that the central values of liberal religion are revealed in varying ways in all the traditions named as Sources. Certainly there is openness among UUs to learning from the various Sources. Or at the very least, there is a willingness by UUs to affirm the parts in the many Sources that serve to support what they already believe. This approach can be likened to the practice of proof-texting, or finding passages out of context that support one's biases. Proof-texting is a fundamental problem in a "cafeteria" style of religion. For example, with proof-texting, a person can read a passage from Confucius alongside one from Jesus to make a point and to demonstrate that both religions are basically pointing to the same ends. However, the core Christian idea of turning the other cheek is antithetical to the strict, hierarchical ethic of Confucianism. Significant and distinct differences and incompatibilities, like the one cited above, rarely get seriously examined when proof-texting is an acceptable and normative practice.

A good example of proof-texting is the Jefferson Bible, wherein through eliminating the parts he did not agree with, Thomas Jefferson created an interpretation of the Christian religion and a version of Jesus that perfectly reflected the values of an 18th century Enlightenment-inspired intellectual. He created a Jesus who reflects the values of Jefferson himself. When fundamentalist Christians pick and choose from the Bible to back up their preconceived beliefs, UUs find the practice infuriating and disingenuous. When UUs do the same thing, it is usually called "liberal religion." Granted, UUs are not claiming to accept the entire Bible literally, yet the essential intellectual and practical problems of proof-texting remain the same in both situations.

Interpreting scripture requires some methodology (also known as a hermeneutic of interpretation). William Ellery Channing, in his formative sermon *Unitarian Christianity*, offered a hermeneutic for interpreting the Bible. However to my knowledge, UUs today do not have, nor do they teach, a hermeneutic for reading scripture(s). The integrity of a religious tradition that claims to draw from many sources would be greatly strengthened if there were some established methodological approaches to guide its members in the ways of credible interpretation. The lack of credible guidelines for interpretation can lead to some pretty incredible beliefs. UUs need guidelines for interpretation that can foster logical consistency, historical accuracy, and theological coherence, ideally leading to moral fruitfulness.

When parishioners ask me why I do not use more of the world's scriptures representationally throughout the year in my preaching and worship, I explain that I do not know enough about all of these scriptures and traditions to use them authoritatively. So, for example, when I speak of a Buddhist idea, my authority in doing so is limited mostly to what it means to me today and is less informed by what it meant in its time and place, and/or what it has meant to believers in our tradition over time, or even what it has meant to believers in its own tradition. I also cannot usually speak to its historic influence on our society. Therefore, without doing extensive research or receiving greater education, when I use other traditions I have uprooted them from their origins, and while that can be instructive and even helpful on some level, it may greatly misrepresent these traditions. At a minimum, UUs need to be honest about what we are doing when we draw from sources of inspiration about which we are only superficially knowledgeable.

Regarding the biblical traditions, UUs have as much of a claim on the Bible's interpretation as anyone. It has been part of the Unitarian and Universalist families (of faith) for centuries. UUs have a tradition of interpretation and experience with these scriptures to draw upon, and UU ministers have at least attained a graduate-level competency in them. Moreover, UUs live in a culture that requires basic biblical literacy for full engagement religiously, politically, intellectually, and rhetorically. The renewal of UUism depends on a rediscovery and reclamation of its primary rootedness in western biblical religion in a way that also remains open to the plethora of ancient and contemporary sources of wisdom and truth.

PROVIDING SPIRITUAL ROAD MAPS

Religious traditions typically have an annual liturgical calendar that includes practices, readings, and rituals based in the stories of scripture. These traditions offer their members a consistent structure and thoughtful direction for the development of religious and spiritual competencies and wisdom. The structure provides both a map and a journey for members, offering them an opportunity to develop an understanding of and aptitude for issues such as forgiveness, redemption, sacrifice, mercy, love, freedom, justice, and resurrection (of the spirit). In other words, they are intentional about teaching the essentials of a spiritually grounded life.

Contemporary UUism lacks any consistent methodology or structure to help ensure that congregations are offering a well-rounded diet of theological learning and practices. Ministers preach on whatever topic they feel like preaching on. In fact, a UU parishioner could sit in a UU church every week for decades and attend Sunday-school classes and never encounter a teaching on redemption or sacrifice or forgiveness or mercy or evil from a liberal religious perspective. In fact, UU ministers and UU congregations are generally ill-equipped to provide consistent and adequate training and education (within their congregations) in the ways of a theologically grounded and spiritually centered life. This deficiency comes in part from a lack of accountability to any scripture or liturgical calendar. The result is a UU movement that claims in theory to draw on many sources, but that fails in practice to organize its offerings in a way that provides clear spiritual road maps for people to grow in wisdom and wholeness. This failure to offer a structured methodology (or spiritual road maps) leaves too much to chance and is largely responsible for the inconsistencies in the experience of UU religion across the nation, despite a unified Statement of Purposes and Principles.

To remedy this deficiency, more and more churches are developing a system of theological themes around which they focus their worship, classes, small groups, and other offerings. The theme-based approach is being pioneered in some of our larger churches such as All Souls in Tulsa; Weston, Massachusetts; and Westshore in Cleveland. Each of these models offers a structure for learning liberal theology and building spiritual depth in a practical everyday context. These churches are intentionally providing a balanced diet of theological learning that fills a need that the laity has been requesting for years.

MISSING PRINCIPLES

Despite the considerable weaknesses outlined above, some people will continue to assert that the Principles are central to UUism and its future. Indeed, the current Commission on Appraisal is in the process of reviewing the Statement with the intention of revising or renewing it. With that task in mind, a number of missing ingredients would, if added, at least help the Principles become a more balanced articulation of the essential values of liberal religion. Missing ingredients include a sense of sacrifice and human sinfulness and human vulnerability, an articulation of the human need to surrender to something larger than oneself, and a commitment to spiritual practice.

Unfortunately, the lack of explicit acknowledgment of sinfulness, sacrifice, and surrender in the current Principles has added to a UU culture that is similar to the way T. S. Eliot once described his Unitarian relatives:

> [To be a Unitarian] was to be noble, upright, and superior to all other human beings . . . . Unitarians believed that they were already enlightened; the enlightenment for them was an intellectual achievement. . . . Unitarians were put on earth to better the lot of humanity, to be a good and inspiring example. . . . Unitarians were expected to be dutiful, benevolent, cheerful, self-restrained and unemotional. . . . They attended church to set a good example to others. (Interdependence, Sec. 5).

UUs have come to downplay the concept of human sinfulness to a fault. It may have begun as an attempt to rectify a strict Calvinist overemphasis on original sin. Yet the reality is that UU churches are filled with people who, in the course of their lives or in the past week, have missed the mark, hurt others or themselves, made mistakes, feel ashamed and guilty, and are in other ways in need of succor as well as in need of modes and tools of redemption. UU worship and theologies need to be able to meet this deep human reality of sinfulness and need to stop covering it over with a happy face.

UUism also needs to be more explicit about what Dietrich Bonhoeffer calls "costing commitments"—the willingness to pay a price for one's commitments. A lack of willingness to sacrifice for one's values undermines one's good intentions.

> The free church is an organization we establish and join so that we may help each other to find, over and over again, in a thousand varying time frames and settings, what are our own worthiest loves, and therefore, what these loves now require of us (1 Wesley, 12).

There is a question whether UUs are willing to "commit to spiritual discipline as deeply as to spiritual freedom" (COA Engaging, 152). Also, are UUs willing to sacrifice financially—to give 10 percent of their income to support the church and other causes that incarnate their values? Are UUs willing to offer the time, talent, and treasure to build congregations and an Association that can offer the world a powerful example of "the beloved community"? Are UUs willing to surrender enough of their individual self-interest to create healthy communities and to allow themselves to be challenged and held accountable by their church? Are individual congregations willing to agree to responsibilities to the larger Association?

> A fundamental problem ... is that the structure of the movement gives much authority but very few concomitant responsibilities to individual congregations. The UUA thus makes virtually no demands, but issues only requests, invitations, or advice for such vital elements as financial support; attendance at General Assemblies and district meetings by appropriate delegates; good working relationships with members of the professional ministry; and wide cooperation among congregations (Interdependence, Sec. 5).

It is difficult to build a high-expectation church that transforms lives and shapes nations within this current structure. In place of being bound together by a set of vague, unimpassioned principles, UUism could be united by a truly living, binding covenant. A covenant by nature involves promise, commitment, and sacrifice. Moreover, truly committing to a covenant requires a degree of surrender to something larger than one's individual self-interest.

> [To summarize James Luther Adams:] Strong, effective, lively liberal churches, capable of altering positively sometimes the direction of their whole society, will be those liberal churches whose lay members can say clearly, individually and collectively, what are their own most important loyalties, as church members. (1 Wesley, 4).

The Principles Statement, as currently written and conceived, is insufficient to foster what James Luther Adams called strong, effective, and lively churches. The Statement does not articulate clearly enough the most important loyalties of Unitarian Universalists. Nor do the Principles effectively bind UUs in covenant.

CONCLUSION

The Unitarian Universalist Association's Principles and Purposes Statement does not contain what is necessary to fashion a people with deep religious sensibilities or informed theological comprehension. Therefore, UUs need to develop ways to create a sense of unified identity in this pluralistic movement that binds UUs together while offering the building blocks for strong, sustaining, theologically and historically rooted congregations and individuals. In an effort to advance this important work, this chapter has outlined five steps.

First, Unitarian Universalist leaders need to do a much better job of clarifying for the movement and their congregations what the Principles

Statement is and is not and how the statement can be used and misused.

Second, much greater clarity and discernment are needed about the Unitarian Universalist tradition's relationship to its many sources, along with a fundamental reclamation of the biblical and scriptural roots of UUism.

Third, UUs need to develop guidelines and a methodology for reading and understanding scripture(s) so that "picking and choosing" involves interpretation and exegesis that have integrity, consistency, coherence, historical accuracy, and moral profitability—in other words, interpretation that involves more than an "it feels good to me" hermeneutic.

Fourth, instead of leaving so much to chance and to the idiosyncrasies of individual ministers and congregation, UUs need to articulate clearer spiritual road maps for their congregations for the fashioning of religiously whole people and communities. Such a process will involve identifying the essential spiritual and theological themes and topics for living a life of love, wisdom and wholeness. Then, it will require congregations to provide a consistent and structured set of offerings through worship, ritual, education, and spiritual practices week after week and year after year. UUism needs something analogous to a liturgical year or lectionary system that is set in a context of freedom of belief and a plurality of resources. By whatever name, the system and process need to offer members an annual cycle of worship and programming that involves essential religious issues such as creation, brokenness, forgiveness, redemption, evil, faith, death, renewal, grace, and more.

Finally, UUs need a clear and binding covenant as a movement, and especially within individual congregations, that inspires true sacrifice and surrender and that includes powerful ways for people to enter the covenant.

A Unitarian Universalist movement with these principal qualities and a strong sense of purpose and identity can be a powerful and transforming force for love and justice in the 21st century.

BIBLIOGRAPHY

Beach, George Kimmich. *Transforming Liberalism: The Theology of James Luther Adams.* Boston: Skinner House Books, 2005.

Collier, Kenneth W. *Our Seven Principles in Story and Verse: A Collection for Children and Adults.* Boston: Skinner House Books, 1997.

Engaging Our Theological Diversity. Commission on Appraisal of the Unitarian Universalist Association, 2005.

Frost, Edward. *With Purpose and Principle: Essays about the Seven Principles of Unitarian Universalism.* Boston: Skinner House Books, 1998.

Gilbert, Richard S. *Building Your Own Theology* (second edition). Boston: Unitarian Universalist Association, 2000.

Hoehler, Judith L. "The Unitarian Universalist Dilemma." *The Unitarian Universalist Christian: A Unitarian Universalist Christian Reader,* vol. 51 and 52, 1996-1997.

Interdependence: Renewing Congregational Polity. Commission on Appraisal of the Unitarian Universalist Association, 1997.

Loehr, Davidson. "Why 'Unitarian Universalism' Is Dying." Theme Talk SUUSI, 21 July 2004, First UU Church of Austin.

Merritt, Barbara. "A Subtle Tyranny," *Unitarian Universalist Voice,* vol. 1, no. 2, summer 1995.

Peebles, Linda Olson. "The Futures Report—Toward a Ministry of Religious Education: A Paradigm Shift in Unitarian Universalism." *Unitarian Universalism Selected Essays 1999,* Unitarian Universalist Ministers Association.

Robbins, Wallace W. "Creeds Are the Enemy of Christ." *The Unitarian Universalist Christian: A Unitarian Universalist Christian Reader,* vol. 51 and 52, 1996-1997.

Scovel, Carl R. "What's a Nice Christian Like You Doing in a Denomination like This?" *The Unitarian Universalist Christian: A Unitarian Universalist Christian Reader,* vol. 51 and 52, 1996-1997.

Shaw, Marvin C. "The Test of the Search Is in What We Find: Religious Humanism, Universal Theism, and Liberal Christianity." *The Unitarian Universalist Christian: A Unitarian Universalist Christian Reader,* vol. 51 and 52, 1996-1997.

Wesley, Alice Blair. "The Lay and Liberal Doctrine of the Church: The Spirit and the Promise of Our Covenant." Minns Lectures 2000-2001 (Lecture 1).
———. "Toward a Covenanted Association of Congregations: On Patterns of Authentic Authority among Free Churches." Minns Lectures 2000-2001 (Lecture 6).

THE PRACTICE GAP

BRET LORTIE

I f faith is believing in something when there's a rational reason to believe and also when there's not, by the time I had finally made my way to my first Unitarian Universalist church I had truly lost my faith. I hadn't lost interest in church or religious community, but certainly all the rest: God, redemption, healing, the power to heal, maybe even love. What continued to draw me to church on Sundays is a mystery to me, a mystery grounded in habit and instinct.

Growing up, my life was rooted in twice-a-week church attendance and daily devotional readings. I think one reason we didn't have a lot of conflict in our church (aside from how best to cut the grass around our lawn sign), was that we were so busy praying. When we were confused, we prayed, as we did when we were ill, or angry, or grateful. Each of these states was a prompt to connect with God on an ongoing basis. Prayer was the heart of spiritual practice; it shaped how we understood ourselves as spiritual practitioners— how to grow, how to be in relationship with each other, how to understand the divine presence in our lives.

Studying scripture, attending church gatherings or camps, and engaging with others were additional means to become better spiritual practitioners of faith. Even the parochial college I attended had a daily "Quiet Hour" built into its schedule to accommodate reflection and scripture study. It gave us something to do with our spiritual lives beyond just thinking about them. While the practice of faith shaped my life, I was, like so many potential Unitarian Universalists, theologically adrift, and when this drifting faith in the Christian message finally petered out, the local Unitarian Universalist church was there to catch me. How many others have our churches, societies, fellowships, and congregations likewise caught?

My first reaction to joining a Unitarian Universalist church was not uncharacteristic for many of our newcomers. I thought: "Wow, it's like college, a community center, and religious fellowship all wrapped up in one, and I never have to graduate and leave!" After college I sincerely missed having intellectual stimulation in my life, and here was an organization that could fill in that gap each Sunday. There was music, too, and coffee!

Church became first, intellectual; second, communal; third, something religious—in that inverted order of importance. I could use the excuse that it was the late 1980s and a strange time in my life, or that I was still young and didn't know better, or that I was "just where I needed to be," but really I think this inversion was a failure of the church itself to present richer ground in which I might plant the seeds of new faith.

It was the church that failed to challenge my priorities as I went through the newcomer class, where all that stood between me and the membership book was a class in Unitarian history and a potluck welcome dinner. It was the church that failed to challenge my notion that I was there for myself and not for others, for it was three years before I was asked to do anything other than sit in a pew and think. It was the church that failed to nudge me, once it had presumably healed the wounds left over from my religious upbringing, back into a life of spiritual practice and renewal.

Falling into the Gap

Getting our religious priorities straight demands that we face the gap we've allowed to develop in the spiritual life of many of our churches. I didn't fully realize the large gap in my own spiritual life until I had enrolled in seminary. I had enjoyed church up to that point and was satisfied with its being "good enough." Yet I was called into religious life partly because I was hungry for more. Then, during my first year of seminary, as I stretched myself personally and spiritually, I found myself falling down a lot. I realized I didn't have an embodied spiritual practice, such as the prayer practice of my youth, on which to rest my burdens when they felt like more than I could handle. I was falling into the practice gap, that space between one's zone of comfort and the suffering that is inevitable when you're pushing the boundaries of your existing framework of spiritual reference.

As I fell into the practice gap, I finally decided to sit down. Then I sat some more. I had long been attracted to Buddhist theology, so I began going to Buddhist sanghas looking not for answers but for an anchor. Sadly, I didn't even consider looking for an answer at my own congregation—a fact I realized only recently. What kept me from searching for a deeper spiritual life in my own church?

My spiritual life deepened concurrently in seminary, where I trained for the ministry, and in my sangha, where I found a teacher who helped me develop a sitting practice and relearn that a spiritual life needs space for the spirit to enter. The gap I had fallen into, I realized, was the same gap through which I might allow the spirit to come back into my life. Don't ask me to define what that looks like or how it works. That's a trap in which Unitarian Universalists love to become ensnared. I can say only that there are realities to our existence beyond words—realities that appear only vaguely rational to human sensibilities. That's what it means to experience something through embodied practice. Words are of the mind; the body can tap into another range of natural experience if we have the patience to listen. This space is experienced through prayer or any number of meditation, yogic, or spiritual disciplines. And it takes work!

My own experience of spiritual insufficiency is not unique among Unitarian Universalists. Others in our congregations are also falling into the practice gap, and instead of coming together in love with common tools or even vocabulary at our disposal, we leave those falling the hardest to act out their difficulties in our communities of faith. Resistance to spiritual growth, for example, is a critical part of the growth process. Bodies and hearts ache, and the mind can rationalize a thousand reasons not to have faith. Currently, however, most of our institutions respond not with remedies, but with platitudes (such as our Seven Principles) and "liberty" clauses, which are seen not as the beginning of a search for personal and institutional truth and meaning, but as the end. The practice gap is therefore more than a personal issue—it is the missing piece in our wider movement today. It is an institutional challenge.

Consider almost every other religious trend, denomination, or community. Adherents pray, meditate, chant, walk, whirl, kneel, eat, or engage in any number of other embodied practices. There are countless Unitarian Universalists who practice their faith in these ways, too. The difference is that these practices are peripheral, even extracurricular for most UUs. Congregations may celebrate a spiritual practice or two during the occasional "pagan Sunday" or other "special service"—but not as liturgy or embodied ritual. It's true that there's probably not a single spiritual practice that is going to catch fire throughout our denomination, coast to coast, but each congregation could engage in a search for a practice its members could do together.

One of the questions on the congregational records that churches send out to prospective ministers asks: "What is your congregation's dominant theology?" A survey usually reveals some kind of answer. What if another question asked: "What is the dominant spiritual practice employed by your congregation?" Does the difficulty in offering such practices stem from disagreement on the meaning behind them? Probably, but that is a flimsy excuse. Each of the practices I've identified is richly nuanced and accessible by different paths. Each one offers many, many paths to transcendence.

Prayers, for example, can be contemplative, meditative, written, spoken, silent, mystical, petitionary, and thankful. How many other different types of prayer are there? How many meditation techniques? People walk, bow, stand, prostrate themselves, sit. There are different ways of keeping kosher, maintaining a Sabbath, making a pilgrimage, showing reverence, engaging in the Five Pillars. We need not agree on the details of spiritual practice to engage in one practice and to share the journey. On some level, we know this. Consider how many theologies we reason our way through on any given Sunday!

If all is holy, everything legitimate, all ways equal, what could possibly be wrong with our utter openness to all directions? Nothing. Nothing, I think, is wrong with the openness. It is the failure to move down one path or another that limits our effectiveness. If we were doing things more effectively, our churches would be overflowing with people being healed of their hurts. If we were doing things more effectively, we would be helping a greater number of people outside our church than inside. If we were doing things more effectively, our saving message would travel to the farthest reaches. The truth is, most of our churches aren't growing. Our social actions are often composed of a handful of truly active people who invite the rest to come along for the ride. Our spirituality groups, when and where they exist, often become closed circles that don't project a message of inclusion. Our message isn't getting out.

It may be a stretch to make a connection between fixing all these wrongs and developing common spiritual practices, but I'm here to stretch. I believe that through spiritual practice the connection between the personal and the institutional comes into focus.

The Hunger

If I didn't see a hunger for spiritual practice in our congregations, I wouldn't be writing this. I'd probably be called to serve the Divine in some other capacity, because it is our hunger for spiritual practice that motivates a large part of my ministry. You can see our hunger in many places. First is the fascination that many Unitarian Universalists have with Buddhism. The path that the Buddha laid out is not one of dogma and creed, although some cultures certainly took it in that direction later on. At its core, Buddhism is non-dogmatic: a practical method to minimize the suffering that arises whenever humans cling to desire. I believe that's why Buddhism resonates so deeply with us: early Buddhism was non-theocentric and laid out a clear path to liberation.

Contemplative prayer is another practice that could catch on with UUs, although many in our churches associate prayer with baggage-laden Christian practices. Still, I am working with Buddhist practice, so I am most qualified to offer an example from Buddhism.

Take as an example the practice of satipatthana—realization of mindfulness—as an example. Through the cultivation of sati (or mindfulness, including ethical conduct, liberality, and the laws of nature) we foster an awareness of the present moment that allows us to recollect our lives, inducing a mind characterized by collectedness and the absence of distraction. Cultivating sati leads to a breadth of focus, even what is called a "boundless" state of mind. There is it: a path, a destination, and a goal, all in one.

One of the more popular hymns in our new supplement reads, "We are going, heaven knows where we are going, but we know within." The opposite is precisely the problem: we don't know where we're going and we don't know what signs will tell us when we get there. "There is no there, there," as I've heard it said. In my life spiritual practice has been an antidote to this fuzziness. In practice one finds clarity, and when my suffering is diminished I experience that clarity as Truth. Goal, path, and discipline are all wrapped into one. Likewise, I believe that our faith, if brought into fuller being through the inclusion of spiritual practices, might offer the world a saving grace the like of which has never been offered.

How would we do this? Since we are theologically pluralistic, our approach to spiritual practice could likewise be pluralistic. We could easily incorporate in our services a significant amount of time for prayer, for example. (And many of us are doing so.) I have found that newcomers don't run screaming from prayer. They expect a little prayer in a church and are moved in a positive way by our manner of praying—in the same way that our mode of preaching is distinctive from that in other Protestant churches. Or we could work toward longer silences in our services instead of the less-than-a-minute gaps we sometimes call "meditation." What would a good five-or ten-minute leap into silence look like for us on a Sunday morning?

We can begin to promote spiritual practice immediately by encouraging the work already being done by our spirituality small groups such as our Christian affinity groups, Buddhist study groups, and Pagan circles, and by creating additional groups based on a model of small-group ministry. By instituting and supporting curious and intentional exploration of communal practices—in the same mode of intentional exploration we have applied to our theologies—our faith might become not only liberal and affirming, but also irresistible and powerful.

Whatever the methods we apply, a next step for Unitarian Universalism is to include in our Sunday gatherings an emphasis on practice. Just as a reasoned faith liberates minds, an embodied faith will liberate the souls entering our doors, souls hungry for what we have to offer.

The Traps

With hunger must come caution, for desire of any kind—even for spiritual practice—is fraught with danger. To eat is nourishing and sustaining. Gluttony can kill you. To strive for excellence is noble. Ambition and greed destroy lives. I don't need to go through the other seven "deadlies" to make my point about life in the here and now: that if we're hungry for spiritual practices that nourish and sustain our lives, we must also watch where we're headed.

The religious scholar and Zen teacher David Loy notes that Western culture is so interested in clinging to something permanent that we cling to the only thing we can: consumerism. We approach spiritual practice the way we approach products, looking for immediate results and believing that more is better. Aside from the temptation to model our church programs after consumer models (which is a different essay), the consumer model when applied to spiritual practice is especially dangerous to our spiritual well-being.

In *Cutting Through Spiritual Materialism*, Buddhist teacher Chogyam Trungpa points out that walking a spiritual path is a subtle process. A spiritual discipline can cut through our confusion, uncover the awakened mind. When it is crowded or controlled by ego, however, it can allow us to deceive ourselves, to begin thinking we are developing spiritually when instead we're merely strengthening our egocentricity. Ego can convert anything to its own use—to the point that, as Trungpa says, we can wind up in the middle of a spiritual junkyard, surrounded by all the pretty practices we've encountered on our spiritual journey, and fed by none of them.

The antidote to this confusion: learning to cherish the most precious pieces of what our journey reveals, to be more discriminating and mindful. How do we know what to cherish? By listening to our instincts, hearing a call, and jumping into the practice gap. We humans cling tightly to our ego-driven understandings, afraid of the empty space before us, afraid we'll find nothing to anchor ourselves as we drift toward an unfixed destination. It takes courage to get lost and simply trust that we'll be found.

My experience tells me that it will take a lifetime to develop and cherish just one or two of the beautiful practices that emerge. Therefore, the point of offering spiritual practice is not to have members dabble with this, and mix and match that. The point is to support people in exploring intentionally a variety of spiritual practices within the church structure, so that the search itself becomes a communal activity.

WE'VE TRIED THIS, HAVEN'T WE?

Unitarian Universalism has already introduced unique practices into our communities of faith. One of these is "joys and sorrows," which can allow a faith community to hold its members' lives in powerful and affirming ways. The sharing of joys and sorrows can draw people tightly into each other's lives. However, many congregations have found that "joys and sorrows" doesn't work well beyond a certain point in a congregation's growth. Many congregations develop a beloved practice of detailed sharing, only to have to abandon it as they grow into a mid-or large-sized church. In a large church, there are just too many people to accommodate within a reasonable amount of time. In any case, joys and sorrows can leave visitors scratching their heads about the reverent meaning of what seems to be a social practice.

Small-group ministry is another practice that UU congregations have embraced. Small ministry groups, or covenant groups, allow members to hold each other's lives—through the practice of cultivated silence, active listening, and nonjudgmental interaction—in a way that most of us do not experience anywhere else in our lives. In most groups, a set of rules and a covenant help participants cultivate a practice that eventually becomes second nature. All constituent partners in a covenant group program— the groups, the individuals in them, and the institutions in which they are embedded—benefit from the interactions that begin and end with the spiritual practice of small-group ministry. In this way, small-group ministry transforms both congregations and individual lives.

Small-group ministry works especially well as a congregation grows in membership. In fact, if everyone in a Unitarian Universalist congregation were involved in small-group ministry, I might never have written this article: that's how powerful I believe the practice to be. On the other hand, I don't expect that everyone in our movement will someday be involved in small-group ministry. Given our pluralism, it just isn't going to appeal to everyone.

Our pluralism is the main reason I am advocating a shift in emphasis for our movement rather than a prescription for everyone's growth. No one spiritual practice is ever going to work for all of us. But a shift in emphasis, a focus on spiritual practice, can enlarge the potential of our churches and transform individual lives. Unitarian Universalists and Unitarian Universalist institutions everywhere should be looking into their lives for those threads that pull them into deeper meaning with existence—with others and with the spirit that grounds our being. If we're not doing that, then we're feeding the mind, but not the soul. And if the business of the church is saving souls (not from damnation but from the many pits and fissures into which our lives can drop), then we ought to be about our job.

Practice with Reason

I came into Unitarian Universalism wanting, among other things, more embodied spirituality in my life. It did such a great job at nurturing those "other things"—such as providing a foundation of faith for my son and empowering me in my personal search for truth and meaning—that I didn't leave. I stayed to carve out a space for embodied practice in this faith that grounds me in so many other ways. It grounds me in its affirmation of the inherent worth of the individual. It grounds me in its affirmation of our connection to each other, without dogma, without creed, without oppressive restrictions. I am afraid, however, that many won't stick around unless our movement embarks on a clearer path toward including spiritual practice in our congregational life. Practice is a way to integrate reason and heart, intellect with inner knowing, personal freedom with the journey we share. This book you hold in your hand is about two things: saving Unitarian Universalism and sharing its redemptive message with every spiritually hungry person who is in need of what we offer. When our religion finds its voice and people come flocking to our doors, what do we offer them?

We welcome the kinds of questions that hold a seeker's attention for a time, and spiritual practice is a way to offer people practical tools to find answers that work in their lives, answers that lead to healing, redemption, and liberation. We offer action and reflection, and spiritual practice adds to that engagement a richer path toward transformation for those who seek to live better lives, lives that matter, lives that are more clearly aimed toward healing and gratitude. This is a world of crushing speed and dehumanizing forces. I believe in the power of spiritual practice to be salve and antidote to those forces. I have come to rest my faith in practice. As a church, as a denomination, as individuals, I pray we will cultivate a similar commitment to practice, which we can then share with all who need it.

MY CONCERN: JOYS AND CONCERNS

TAMARA LEBAK

Joy can be real only if people look upon their life as a service,
and have a definite object in life outside themselves and
their personal happiness.

—LEO NIKOLAEVICH TOLSTOY

My ministerial training was generous with stories about churches labeled "dysfunctional." However, it did not specifically address methods or theory to help ministers to support those churches to become healthier systems. In fall 2005, I began a postgraduate study program at the Gestalt Institute of Cleveland Organization and Systems Development Center. I wanted to be equipped to understand church systems. Healthy church systems in particular have interested me since I left my home church, First Unitarian, Dallas, to attend seminary. I wanted to know how I could translate my experience of that large church to other church settings. Although I would not assume that size determines health, I would argue that growth is a byproduct of a healthy church system. What can churches of all sizes learn from the commonalities of our large church systems?

WHAT MAKES A CHURCH HEALTHY?

We are an association of congregations, and I would argue that at our best we are churches in association. The word *church* in the New Testament is translated from the Greek word *ekklesia*, which comes from the words *ek*, meaning "out," and *kaleo*, meaning "to call." An *ekklesia* or "calling out" was

109

not just a congregation of people. It was a gathering of those called out to serve God. In church we are called out to seek beyond the self. In church we are called to remember that we are not alone in our common story of being human and being alive. We gather with one essential value we hold in common: that there is something larger than ourselves in this world that we are called to serve. The role of the church is for each of us to call out, "Here I am," bringing our gifts to a greater mission and purpose. In church we are asked to bring our whole selves to the table and then to balance our wants and needs with a common purpose. That common purpose ought to be articulated in every congregation's mission and vision. It ought to be modeled in a church's public worship, demonstrated in a church's committee meetings, and lived out in the lives of the church members.

Change is a necessary part of all institutions, including churches. What makes a church healthy or unhealthy is directly related to how a church manages change. Healthy churches have clear identities and identified processes for change. To make choices regarding a change, the church must first have a clear understanding of its own identity: how it sees itself and how it is seen in the community and the wider movement. We must first know where we are before we can know where we are going. One reason is that if intentional change is to be successful, change initiatives must always support the mission and vision of the church and be congruent with the church's identity. Healthy churches promote transparent processes to determine when to act on a change initiative and how to implement the change. Such a process requires having systems in place that resist vocal minorities who rally for special interests that do not benefit the institution's mission and vision. So that my assumptions might be more visible, I have created a chart that highlights some of the issues that may affect churches in managing change and how those behaviors fall into the healthy or unhealthy category.

HEALTHY CHURCHES ⬇	UNHEALTHY CHURCHES ⬇
Have clear vision, mission, and identity.	Vision, mission, and identity are always in flux or nonexistent.
Ownership and congregational buy-in of churchwide covenant of membership.	Membership responsibilities unclear.
Groups within the church covenant explicitly with one another about group membership responsibilities.	Groups within the church have implicit covenant with group members or no covenant at all.
Process for accepting and implementing change is transparent.	Process for accepting and implementing change is unclear or protected.
Power is delegated to those who think both institutionally and individually.	Power is co-opted or granted to a vocal minority, the largest giver(s), or special interest groups, and is focused on individual or small-group wants and needs.
Resistance is seen as a healthy part of the change process, and there is a process for it to be heard and incorporated.	Resistance is seen as a reason to abandon the initiative.
Decisions are made for the health of the whole.	Groups or individuals compete for control of resources and identity and to direct the whole.
Systems are in place to support change.	No systems are in place to support change, or systems that are in place actually prevent change.
Need for change is widely understood and shared (supports mission, vision, and identity).	Change occurs in the name of inclusion, for the sake of appeasing a vocal minority, to avoid conflict, or because change itself is held up by the church as a value rather than a means to an end (lack of mission, vision, and identity).

Healthy Churches ⬇	Unhealthy Churches ⬇
Participants in the change process are aware of their own wants, needs, biases, privileges, and assumptions, and are looking for a win-win.	Participants in the change process are not aware of their own wants, needs, biases, privileges, and assumptions, and are looking for a personal victory or a win-lose.
Benchmarks and objectives are explicit and agreed upon for accountability.	Benchmarks and objectives are subjective and implicit.
Feedback and learning are included at all levels of the process.	Feedback is discouraged or mobilized only by constituency of resistance. Only negative feedback taken into account, no holistic feedback process.
Culture of accountability: mistakes are acknowledged and owned.	Culture of blame, shame, and scapegoating.
Identified leadership is given authority to lead.	Leadership has no actual authority; roles are perfunctory.
Strong commitment from all key constituents to invest in success of the change.	A few players drive or block the change process.
Administrative, ministerial, and lay leadership practices complement and reinforce the change.	Administrative, ministerial, and lay leadership practices prevent and/or stymie the change.
Opportunities for acknowledgement of loss of what was the old way (loss of the familiar, people places, routines, etc.). Intentional grief process.	Focus is only on the new way.
Tradition is engrained in identity that continues to serve longtime and current constituency (ritual, liturgy, etc.), and supports identity.	No identifiable or sustained tradition, or traditions that insulate or exclude.
Outside perspective invited for major change initiatives to encourage whole system accountability.	Whole system accountability is discouraged.

A commitment to a church creates opportunities to live out our values. The individual benefits of this commitment are many: we are strengthened, encouraged, shown compassion; we are seen and heard, and our individual stories are known. Unfortunately, these byproducts are often confused as the purpose of the church. In our agreeing to come together *as a church*, we have agreed to direct our attention and our gifts toward serving our highest calling. At its best, church offers us an opportunity to demonstrate our values, to model healthy boundaries, and to have our thoughts and actions challenged. Through our association with the church we are called out to be our best selves. Through worship, ritual, and our relationships we are drawn toward a vision of the world that we can hold in common as a community. One powerful way we articulate our identity is through our corporate worship.

CASE IN POINT: JOYS AND CONCERNS

I am shocked by the many churches in our movement that cling to "Joys and Concerns" in worship, especially in the name of inclusion. In its most common form, "Joys and Concerns" is an open-mic sharing in the middle of a corporate public worship service, and serves as the model spiritual practice of unhealthy churches. The church's primary opportunity to define itself as a single corporate body with a common vision is in its public worship. This unscripted and unpredictable practice speaks volumes about what is most important to us. It clouds the worship message, gives power to a vocal minority, and focuses the entire church inward on personal matters. The effect of Joys and Concerns on a whole church system is not the same as it would be in a small group.

In a small-group setting, the benefits of Joys and Concerns are numerous. The practice helps to reinforce a small group's identity by focusing on the individuals that make up the group. Yet the purpose of a small group is different from that of a church. Small groups facilitate intimacy and build relationships. Beyond helping form a small group's identity, the practice of Joys and Concerns mostly serves to keep groups small and perpetuates unhealthy church system behaviors. Arguments for continuing this practice in public worship do not take into account the actual result to the system. I will walk through some of the more common claims and highlight the actual system result. Most of the claims for the value of Joys and Concerns point to real needs in the system. I will sort the church need from the claim and then offer examples of how healthy church systems have successfully accommodated the need. The information is summarized in the following chart.

CLAIM: JOYS AND CONCERNS IN PUBLIC WORSHIP ... ➡	ACTUAL SYSTEM RESULT ➡
Offers opportunity for individuals to participate in worship	Gives power to vocal minority. Muddies the worship message.
Informs congregation about items missed in announcements.	Gives power to vocal minority, Muddies the worship message.
Informs minister and congregation of pastoral concerns.	Assumes all are equally equipped to respond. Encourages unhealthy boundaries by promoting unrealistic expectations of a cor-porate response to personal concerns.
Creates intimacy within congregation.	Holds up in high esteem one way of emotional vulner-ability that caters to the extrovert. With no actual corporate response possible, promotes surface-level engagement from the majority of the congregation and creates false sense of intimacy.
Models our value of inclusion.	Treats corporate body as a small group made up of those who speak and those who directly respond to speakers after the service. Devalues worship leader roles. Forces corporate attention on personal issues.
Models our value of compassion.	Encourages surface-level engagement from majority of the congregation.
Creates opportunities to share.	Encourages culture of vulnerability without intimacy.

REAL NEED HIDDEN WITHIN THE CLAIM ➡	EXAMPLES FROM HEALTHY CHURCH SYSTEMS
Individual participation in corporate worship.	Singing, calling out of names, lighting of candles with music, responsive or collective reading, flower communion, and other rituals.
Improved process for disseminating information and announcements.	Multiple opportunities that provide the same message: Newsletter, vetted spoken announcements, printed announcements, designated announcement area, website, reinforced deadlines.
Improved process for gathering, disseminating, and responding to pastoral information.	Lay-led pastoral care team, prayer box, pastoral prayer, small-group ministry, designated voicemail or response line, access to the minister.
Intimacy among membership. Opportunities for individual vulnerability and personal disclosure.	Small group ministry, intentional small group check-in at programs, pastoral prayer, vetted ministerial vulnerability. Vulnerability from the minister who is delegated to speak on behalf of the church creates whole-group intimacy.
Trust building with worship leader. Other means to include examples of healthy boundaries.	Clear paths to membership, trans-parent processes of involvement, lay and ministerial leadership demonstrates inclusiveness, designated persons to welcome and greet.
Multiple opportunities for members to demonstrate compassion.	Shawl ministry, small groups, lay-led pastoral care team, organized food support, service opportunities, card-writing ministry, etc.
Opportunities for vulnerability within developed relationships or with trained responders.	Small-group ministry, lay-led pastoral care team, small-group churchwide engagement.

The arguments for having Joys and Concerns in the worship service include:

1. Joys and Concerns offers an opportunity for individuals to participate in the worship service.
2. It serves as a vehicle for disseminating pastoral information and the business of the church.
3. It creates intimacy.
4. It models our common values of inclusion, compassion, and the worth of the individual.

In fact, the impact of Joys and Concerns on a system—that is, on any system larger than a small group—serves to counter the important needs hidden within these claims. The needs of healthy and unhealthy church systems are similar. Most churches want to provide opportunities for individuals to participate in worship. Most churches want to communicate well, facilitate intimacy among their members, and demonstrate compassion and the values held in common. The difference is that healthy church systems meet these needs through practices that take into account the mission and vision of the church, the needs of the membership, the health of the church system, and the eyes of the stranger. In healthy church systems, worship is done in ways that are welcoming to outsiders. Worship is indicative of the integrity of the overall church system.

Changing our Concern

How does a church that has Joys and Concerns begin to shift to something different? That depends on the church and the leadership. How long has the practice been in place? What does this part of the service represent to the various constituencies in the congregation? What is the need behind the desire to keep this practice? Is there a constructive way to have the conversation needed in order to make the change? All of the answers depend on the health of the congregation. How are decisions made? What systems are in place to support the change? Is the need for change widely understood? Could you use this chapter to begin a conversation? Are those who would be needed to facilitate the change aware of their own wants, needs, and assumptions? Are those involved in the conversation looking for a win-win? The previous chart on healthy church behaviors may serve as a starting point.

Let's assume that the change initiative supports the mission, vision, and identity of the church, and has buy-in from key constituencies, and that the church leadership practices complement and reinforce the change.

What comes next? Grief and resistance will be a natural part of any change process. Change takes place from the inside out—it is personal and involves emotional, social, and psychological dynamics. Functional resistance involves progressing through the stages of grief and naming what will be lost by the change initiative and what the new reality will be.

Unfortunately, the stages of grief (denial, anger, bargaining, etc.) may appear at first to be dysfunctional resistance. Symptoms of dysfunctional resistance include stagnation at a particular stage, withdrawal from the community, or behavior that seeks to undermine the leadership. Successful change initiatives proceed at a pace that brings along key constituencies and allows space for others to move through the stages. It aims to understand those who are seeking to prohibit the change without enabling a disrespect of the process. Other resistance that is not dysfunctional is best handled through opportunities to talk about the change and its impacts and reactions, as well as through acknowledgment of what is gained and what is lost. In other words, a process is created that allows for the important work of letting go.

As with grief of all kinds, sometimes what is being lost extends far beyond the immediate context of the current change initiative. Change often triggers reactions connected to other losses. When the resistance becomes personal, the appropriate response is pastoral and not institutional. Too often church leaders attempt to fix personal or idiosyncratic concerns by making institutional changes. Red flags often include behavior or emotional investment that appears oversensitive, overly forceful, or simply out of context. The benefit of the minister's leading the change process is that he or she often has pastoral information and history that can inform the understanding of an out-of-the-ordinary reaction. Ministers, with their ability to know a congregation pastorally and to lead an organization through change, must balance the personal and the institutional.

For the success of our churches, we need ministers who are intentional about their own change theory. It would be wise to begin to include education in systems-change theory in UU seminary training, and for the UU process of fellowshipping ministers to require articulation and demonstration of change practices. In the meantime, it is important for churches that become disrupted by change to be encouraged to seek outside consultants. Professionals from the UUA and the Alban Institute can be invaluable in helping churches to navigate needed change. Ministers with a variety of experience and those trained in systems theory can also support a church's move through a major change. Our movement depends on the success of our unhealthy churches moving to healthy systems and practice. Even I would light a candle to that!

UNITARIAN UNIVERSALIST OUTREACH AND INREACH

REFLECTIONS ON THE POTENTIAL OF NEW TECHNOLOGIES

Erik David Carlson

Imagine an American woman who is in her mid-20s and living in the Middle East. Although she was raised Catholic, she has lost touch with her religious roots and has not considered returning to religion until the conflicts in her current place of residence compel her to seek spiritual guidance and community. In a single Google search, she finds the Church of the Younger Fellowship, a website community that speaks about liberal religion and the principles of Unitarian Universalism. She returns to the site a few days later and signs up with a member account. Before she knows it, she is linked to a community of likeminded individuals for whom distance is no object.

Consider a man who grew up Unitarian Universalist and still identifies as UU, but who has not attended a service since early in high school. One day at work he is browsing the internet and finds FUUSE.com, a media repository and community website made up of a large population of Unitarian Universalists. A few weeks after he signs up, an old friend from his high school youth group contacts him through the site and encourages him to check out a local congregation with a good reputation. Less than a month later, he attends his first UU service in 20 years. The next week, he takes his family with him.

Finally, picture a very angry and lonely teenager. She spends most of her time at home on her computer, isolated from her parents and siblings. Though her family isn't religious, an online friend has suggested that she check out FUUSE.com, because she might find some of the people and discussions interesting. She does so, and she meets people easily through the site. For the first time she speaks at length about her spiritual beliefs regarding God, an afterlife, and what determines a moral life. She feels connected and cared for. A year later, she attends her first UU service, followed by a youth group meeting. Several months later, her entire family follows her lead and begins to attend.

All three of these stories describe real people in real situations who found or reconnected with Unitarian Universalism through websites that I helped to build and operate. While most seekers' paths to Unitarian Universalism are not quite as simple as the ones described here, the internet is fast becoming the single most important purveyor of information in the world. Increasingly, it should be considered Unitarian Universalism's greatest outreach tool. Over the past six years I have had the good fortune to be part of several projects that use technology to foster communication among Unitarian Universalists around the world. I have had to learn more than I ever thought I would need to know about web design and user interfaces, but I have seen firsthand the amazing potential for community building through the internet and new media. As invested as we Unitarian Universalists are in creating spiritual community, we owe it to ourselves to make use of the technologies that will help us bring our message to those who are part of the technological future and to those who are currently in need.

BROADCAST MEDIA TOOLS

We can begin with the familiar. Broadcast media have been effective modes of communication for more than 50 years. I remember watching Saturday morning cartoons as a child and being exposed to several public service announcements provided by the Church of Jesus Christ of Latter Day Saints (the Mormons). Conversely, I am certain I never saw a single liberal religious ad. Similarly, any contemporary digital cable television package offers multiple channels that feature conservative Christian evangelicals, while alternative spiritual messages are elusive at best. We as Unitarian Universalists need to correct this imbalance, to water the spiritual broadcast desert so that the spirit of open inquiry can flourish.

While owning a cable network is probably not feasible for the UUA alone, the spirit of pluralism and collaboration in which Unitarian Universalism is grounded should allow us to consolidate resources with other national religious and advocacy organizations with which we are already partners. The names that immediately come to mind are organizations such as the

United Church of Christ, the American Friends Service Committee, and the Interfaith Alliance. Together, such a collection of organizations could put together high-quality programming that discusses local and national news items from the liberal religious perspective, gives coverage to protests and social justice programs too often ignored by the national corporate media, and provides an open forum for evaluation of justice issues that pervade our country, such as systemic racism and the ever-widening class divide.

Liberal religious organizations such as the UUA can also employ radio broadcasts as a less expensive alternative to television. Some UU churches like the First Church of Boston, broadcast Sunday services on local or college radio, but as of this writing there are none that appear on a national feed. New radio broadcast options include fledgling HD (high-definition) and satellite radio stations, some of which are still in search of programming. These present yet another opportunity for collaboration with liberal religious partners to reach a national audience.

Web Marketing is Passive Marketing

Advertising and marketing are touchy subjects for many Unitarian Universalists. Direct marketing of faith, for some, can conjure images of traditional evangelism, in which religious ideals are all too often imposed upon people through political power rather than genuine piety. The mere notion of cold-calling or ringing doorbells to advertise one's faith leaves many a UU feeling queasy. Now, because of new technology, we do not have to sell Unitarian Universalism door to door to make our message known. Several forms of passive marketing can help us reach a broad range of people without resorting to anything that resembles the Madison Avenue hard sell or the invasive proselytizing of some other traditions.

Websites are among the most effective forms of passive marketing. Even very simple congregational websites can be effective, because they offer a passive but immediately available source of information. The North Shore Unitarian Church in Deerfield, Illinois (*http://nsuc.org*), First Unitarian Church of Oakland, California (*http://www.uuoakland.org*), and First Unitarian Church of Albuquerque, New Mexico (*http://www.uuabq.org*), are all good examples of clean, professional, and attractive websites that not only help visitors find where the church meets also but invite them to participate. People who are not interested in finding church websites will probably not stumble across one for a UU congregation, but those seeking a place to worship are likely to look for churches online. Well-crafted key words like "religious community" and "spirituality" in website header information, combined with link sharing with other UU churches and organizations, can quickly put a local congregation's website near the top of a Google search for "religion" in its area and create an increase in visitors almost immediately. If they feel invited, visitors to websites can quickly become visitors to services—and then potential members. Remember, of course, that a website cannot do everything for a church: once a website has gotten visitors through the door, it is up the church community to make them feel welcome and invite them to return.

Outreach

Despite evidence suggesting that websites are crucial to contemporary outreach, many churches have not dedicated the resources necessary to create and maintain a viable public presence on the internet. They rely instead on volunteers for design, initial content, and maintenance. At first thought this route might seem reasonable and cost-effective. Many people know how to build websites, after all. But UU congregations benefit from the flexibility and functionality of professionally designed websites, rather than sites built by amateurs. Flexible, up-to-the-moment sites will not only express our values but also allow us to capture and capitalize upon new media and communication trends.

When consulting with churches that are resistant to hiring professional staff to design and implement internet technology, I have often used the analogy of a major building project. If a congregation has outgrown its sanctuary and needs an addition to its existing building, would it have a volunteer member who happened to take an architecture course in college design it? Would the congregation establish a "construction committee" of member volunteers to pour concrete, run electrical wiring, and hang drywall? And finally, if the addition was going to cost $50,000, would members simply ignore their need, or would they start a capital campaign, knowing that it might take some time to raise the funds? My point is that we are now living in a world where internet technology is developing quickly and the understanding of internet users is far more savvy than it was even five years ago. People do not spend time on websites that are hard to navigate or difficult to read. Another website is just a click away, as modern internet users are abundantly aware.

Some visionary UU churches have indeed begun using new media to great effect. Podcast UU sermons are already quite popular, and some churches upload videos of sermons and even entire services. A recent search of the iTunes podcast listing confirmed that there are more than 100 UU churches that podcast or archive their shows on the internet, including the First Unitarian Society of Madison, Wisconsin; the First Parish of Concord, Massachusetts; and All Souls Unitarian Church in Tulsa, Oklahoma. An increasing number of these are making financial and technical investments to share their message for the greater good, as well as to attract visitors. Like websites, podcasts are available to the public without being invasive: people who want them can simply click and find the sermon they want to hear. Although many people who listen to podcast sermons will probably never sign a membership book at a UU church, some inevitably will, and all will have been exposed to a liberal religious message they might otherwise not have experienced.

INREACH

One of the most exciting developments in today's communication technology landscape is one that not only allows churches to advertise themselves and their messages to a larger audience, but also helps their members interact with one another. Password-protected member websites have started to appear throughout the UUA, and these have facilitated church, communal, and social-action events, committee communication, and participation in services and small-group ministries. Both the UU Church of Greater Lynn, Massachusetts (*http://uucgl.org*), and The First Unitarian Church of Orlando, Florida (*http://fuconet.org*), house their committee minutes, membership directories, budget information, and member journals in a password-protected section of their websites.

As congregations grow, person-to-person communications that might otherwise become unwieldy can go online and thrive. "Joys and Sorrows" (also referred to by many churches as "Joys and Concerns"), for example, can be problematic and inappropriate to incorporate into services for many congregations. A "Joys and Sorrows" Web page on a congregational website can allow members to share in detail their important personal events while simultaneously eliminating this burden from the Sunday service. The Church of the Younger Fellowship (*http://uucyf.org*) has taken this potential even further. Its members have developed an online pastoral care team whose job it is to seek out those in need and to make itself immediately available to members as issues arise.

Finally, there is a great environmental and economic benefit for congregations that can save paper, printing, and mailing costs by transitioning to e-mail newsletters, announcements, and membership directories. Technologically savvy congregations generally have an easier time in canvassing, and congregations able to accept credit cards through their websites for recurring pledge payments are much more likely to have a higher percentage of pledges met than churches that do not implement online payment options. By using technology for inreach as well as outreach, Unitarian Universalists may be able to enjoy significant growth in the number of visitors to services, in communication among members, and in our ability to care for members of our congregations.

GENERATION NEXT

An interesting phenomenon is occurring just below the surface among today's youngest voting citizens. According to a January 2007 documentary by PBS titled *Generation Next: Speak Up, Be Heard*, the all-important 16 to 25-year-old segment of our American population is the most liberal-thinking and diverse group in our collective history. Of all the living generations, this one proves to be the most supportive of interracial dating, same-sex unions, and religious tolerance. Its members are voting more than young citizens have ever voted, and they do more community service and volunteer work than any other group in America today.

This segment of the populace is also the most comfortable with technology and alternative media. Largely as a result of this generation's participation, online repositories of shared audio and video media such as YouTube.com are currently the fastest-growing websites on the internet. Although the advent of Tivo, HD digital cable, and satellite TV services have postponed the heralded death of television, growing numbers of "Generation Next" rely almost exclusively on the internet to meet their entertainment, information, and communication needs.

This development means that those who are on the cutting edge of communication technology are also statistically the most likely to be in agreement with and receptive to the Unitarian Universalist message. These trends are echoed within Unitarian Universalism itself. Youth and young-adult UUs contribute mightily to UU-driven sites like FUUSE.com (2,900 members) and to UU groups on secular websites like MySpace.com (1,900 members), LiveJournal.com (1,200 members), and most recently, FaceBook. com (3,100 members). They also respond in record numbers to the Church of the Larger Fellowship's young-adult ministry and its online congregation, the Church of the Younger Fellowship (*http://uucyf.org*). Launched on an incredibly small budget at GA 2005, by this writing the CYF has seen growth at a rate of five members a week. By fall of 2007, it had a membership of 525, representing twelve countries on five continents.

Yet young adults are the least represented in our current congregations. Our failure to engage younger members of our community is compounded by the fact that we retain only a tiny percentage of our graduating high school seniors, though many of them will identify as Unitarian Universalist for the rest of their lives. Unitarian Universalism has an obligation to care for the children raised in its congregations, youth groups, and religious education programs. The care we extend, moreover, is likely to benefit the movement as a whole. By reaching out via technological avenues with which our youth are comfortable, and indeed expert, we can begin not only to communicate with younger UUs but also to attract them as co-creators of our movement. We can give them the voice and the power they will require if they are to carry Unitarian Universalism forward with them into the future.

CONCLUSION AND CALL

In the last decade there has been a surge of radical-right religious organizations that have successfully advanced conservative political agendas despite the fact that these positions are not supported by the majority of Americans. As a result, we have become a more polarized populace, entrenched in a long and devastating war that has in some circles been justified by the religious differences between our predominantly Christian culture and the Islamic theocracies with which we find ourselves in political conflict. People in general, and young people in particular, have begun to equate religion with this specific conservative perspective. "I'm *spiritual* but not *religious*" is a phrase uttered all too often in today's America by citizens of all ages. But as Unitarian Universalists know, we offer a legitimate and compelling alternative to the religious right's perspective: a tradition grounded in principles of pluralism, inclusiveness, civic responsibility, and love. The time has never been more opportune nor the obligation more pressing to express and invite others to embrace the principles of our tradition. We need to reach out in person, in print, and in every way we can—including the use of technology.

It is by using all of the tools available to us that we might truly establish Unitarian Universalism as a recognized and important contributor to the spiritual well-being of our world.

LET US BE AWAKENED

Joseph Santos-Lyons

He who knows not and knows not he knows not: he is a fool—
*   shun him.*
He who knows not and knows he knows not: he is simple—
*   teach him.*
He who knows and knows not he knows: he is asleep—
*   wake him.*
He who knows and knows he knows: he is wise—
*   follow him.*

—Persian apothegm, Sanskrit saying.

The 1997 General Assembly resolution to address our internalized racism is perhaps the most powerful racial-justice initiative we have ever undertaken. We have evolved in our relationship with the oppressed, becoming less interested in charity that maintains the status quo and more interested in empowerment, equality, and reconciliation. We've begun to direct our questioning spirit internally over the years, asking who we are and how we can be authentic to our values in our attitudes and practices.

And still, many people, particularly persons of color and young people in our congregations, express disappointment and a degree of resentment at how they are treated. This is a reality that we need to understand better. Social change is happening slowly in the Unitarian Universalist Association (UUA), and yes, I believe the arc of the universe is long and bends toward justice, but there are times when it feels as though it bends more slowly among us justice-makers. We are reluctant to gaze long and hard at ourselves in a faith that looks so powerfully outward. We are surprisingly dismissive of those not in our presence, often assuming a degree of superiority and projecting an inferiority onto "other" people. When those minorities do appear, we are skeptical, tokenizing, or both, creating a poor environment for their spiritual growth.

Young adults have always been leaders in North American Unitarian Universalism. Ralph Waldo Emerson, Thomas Starr King, and Olympia Brown advanced our living tradition in their 20s, and in modern times many ministers have significantly influenced our spiritual DNA in their young-adult years. As we live longer, we must not neglect or minimize the wisdom of our young prophets. Youth is too often attacked in our society and congregations. Identities—particularly of race, sexual orientation, and economic expression—are woven into this assault, offering snap criticisms which have also served to undermine the dignity of young people. The voices of our youth and young adults need to be cultivated into strong leadership that can help ground our theology and vision for the future.

Everywhere I go, members of the younger generation of Unitarian Universalists are asking about the meaning of identity, wondering about the purpose of our congregations, and making a commitment to engage their own privilege. There is something special here. We have a whole new generation of ministers of color, many of whom made connections with one another as young adults. Their numbers, in which I include myself, are significant. We also have a strong collective of ministers who met as youth and young adults, and who have been shaped by the anti-oppression work led by Continental Unitarian Universalist Young Adult Network (C∗UUYAN) and Young Religious Unitarian Universalists (YRUU).

These relationships are important. They will help our community form a vision and encourage new ideas when the challenges to social justice are difficult and painful. I see a future UUA with a strong, identity-positive, radically inclusive, and spiritually alive leadership.

In three areas of Unitarian Universalism the experience and imagination of youth are fundamental: spiritual practice and discipline, community building, and justice-making. These broad areas were claimed by the Unitarian Universalist young adult movement C∗UUYAN, a sponsored organization of the UUA in the late 1990s, as their core mission. Since then, several relevant and sensitive questions have emerged. Who are we in the global, postmodern information age? What is our religious vision of identity as it relates to war and peace, oppression and justice, suffering and joy? How does our faith respond to the teaching and understanding being championed by our youth on issues of identity?

I've been part of a group of young people who have paid particular attention to issues of race and racism. In this context, we've asked the following questions: How can we transform ourselves into an anti-racist, anti-oppressive, multicultural institution? What ministries are needed for persons of color, multiracial families, adoptees of color, and young people of color? Is Unitarian Universalism hostile to people of color? In a faith with only a handful of active ministers of color a generation ago, and now more than 50 in congregations and communities, with a handful entering the ministry *each year*, will there be a home, love and care, and a professional future for these trailblazers?

X X X

I've been amazed at the identity-positive atmosphere of the younger generation. It seems to run counter to the conservative "just be American" and the liberal "we're all the same" refrains. Young adults of my generation grew up in the post-1960s identity and dignity movements of women, gays and lesbians, and people of color. These young adults lived with multiculturalism in new forms—influenced by media, literature, and social-justice movements that reshaped our attitudes toward difference and diversity. While we haven't fully named, much less overcome, the internalization and institutionalization of white supremacy, patriarchy, heterosexism, ableism, and so forth, I see the younger generation moving toward a more healthy identity-positive consciousness. The most common response I hear from adults in Unitarian Universalism is fear—at the complexity, the stakes, and the expectation of change. The Rev. William Sinkford noted in his controversial *Oregonian* article during General Assembly 2007 another possible dynamic—pride and self-centeredness from front-line activism in the 1960s. "Many of us thought we were going to solve racism and poverty," said Sinkford, who is African American. "To come to terms with the unfinishedness of that work is almost acknowledging a failure for my generation."

The Unitarian Universalist message on identity is falling short in our congregations and the world. We have the wisdom and leadership to elevate our identity-based ministry, and yet significant forces push against this socially complex and spiritually demanding work. I've observed that ministers continue to be trained and ordained without high-quality anti-oppression training and with limited experience when it comes to relationships of accountability with people of color. Those who do maintain a healthy diet of training and accountability in regard to anti-oppression have reported feeling marginalized in their ministerial chapters and congregations, without a strong support network.

Ministers, our called and professionally trained leaders, are now expected to show general competency in anti-oppression ministry, which is a significant step established by the Ministerial Fellowship Committee (MFC). My concern, however, is that the comprehensive training and evaluation are still inconsistent and inadequate. High-quality training, I believe, encompasses three points:

- The ability to understand the diverse impacts of identity on human suffering and joy, including the powers of privilege, inferiority, and internalization.

- Explicit experience addressing an issue of institutional oppression and an ability to articulate the power of institutions in shaping identity, culture, and justice.

- A consciousness of Unitarian Universalist efforts for anti-oppression and a valuing of lifelong engagement with accountability and personal spiritual growth in this area of ministry.

I applaud the efforts of those engaged at this time, and I am gratified by new developments such as annual training for seminarians, funded gatherings for ministers of color, and the establishment of Allies for Racial Equity. We seem to be on the right track, with one exception—coherence. The UUA's Journey Towards Wholeness (JTW) Transformation Committee has stated repeatedly that it does not have the resources to fulfill its mission of guiding the ongoing anti-oppression efforts, and the UUA has devolved significantly from the rough core of ten multiracial, multicultural, and intergenerational staff who supported the JTW initiative. The effort to integrate the responsibilities into all staff portfolios failed to maintain the responsibility of leadership for the initiative. Relationships between projects and programs, such as anti-racism training, congregational justice-making, people of color ministry, and curriculum development have atrophied, and the ensuing level of confusion is an example of institutional control. The synergy that led to the 1997 JTW Resolution, and the subsequent community-based efforts for education, organizing, and accountability seem to be missing today. In their place is an array of excellent work by excellent people—efforts made feeble by poor communication, favoritism, and a lack of shared vision.

While many of our congregations continue to be dominantly white racially, 10 percent are experiencing significant change demographically. While no real statistics are available, I have seen from my travels and ministry with young people more than 100 congregations with growth in adoptees of color, who have added to our multicultural mix that often has its roots in our acceptance of multiracial families. Dozens of these congregations have responded to grassroots efforts to develop places of ministry, such as retreats, to better understand the dynamics, issues, and areas of growth around identity in personal, familial, and community contexts. Yet there is a real struggle, with many members, particularly persons of color, continuing to express a feeling of marginalization and tokenization.

The Unitarian Universalist Association and our congregations, despite active and often effective justice-making efforts, continue to minimize risk to their power by strictly controlling leadership development. Community-based efforts to nurture the religious voice of young Unitarian Universalists have failed to receive significant financial and professional support. Experiments to support spiritual growth with youth of color, global-justice organizers, and anti-violence young adults, have often been met with cynicism, silence, and an inability to understand and handle the tension and conflict that arise from this social-change ministry. I've witnessed how this behavior suppresses the creative, activist, and religious impulses of our young people, in favor of a risk-averse, liability-centered, power-maintenance system. One of the best examples is the Report of the Special Review Commission probing the events surrounding the 2005 General Assembly and the Youth of Color Leadership Development Conference held preceding it. Not only was the report insufficient; it failed to state the ongoing value of leadership development for young persons of color in its recommendations. It focused UUs basically on the need to "appreciate diversity" and offered a distracting emphasis on the wearing of name tags.

Despite my assertion that the UUA and our congregations are not responding well to the leadership of young people, our youth and young adults have grown in confidence to speak up for themselves and for the world. Connections made through various efforts among youth and identity groups have been sustained. This is a testament not only to useful technologies but to thoughtful, inspirational, and dedicated leadership that has advanced Unitarian Universalism. Events and organizations such as Youth of Color Leadership Development, Queer Youth Leaders, Multiracial Families, Transracial Adoptees, the Transgender Workshop for Young Adults, Seminarians of Color, the Young Women's Caucus, and the Cultural Appropriation in Worship Workshop are all examples of recent efforts led by youth and young adults. These have been transformative for participants yet have met their share of challenges. There has been disappointment when institutions rush to judge at the first sign of conflict or resistance. Too often the result of such judgment is the termination, reorganization, or underfunding of important projects.

The resistance can be hard to recognize, yet I believe it is there. For example, over the last 25 years, four efforts to establish a UUA curriculum on racial justice have never been completed. Various explanations have been given—for example, lack of funding, changing racial dynamics, analysis and inclusivity, and staffing changes. People of color working at the UUA have experienced animosity and have suffered the effects of continual reorganization of racial-justice efforts, generally in response to concerns raised from the change that racial justice inspires. There was a period when the UUA Faith in Action Department was eliminated and several staff members of color left under various circumstances. No new staff people were hired immediately to replace them. Several consultants took their place, and for those of us left in the institution, there was a sudden lack of mentoring, internal support, and encouragement. I experienced this outcome directly. These departures and staffing gaps also have the effect of losing institutional knowledge and limiting our ability to develop best practices through learning from our experiences.

I'm at the cusp of "young adulthood" and am beginning to fall out of touch with the realities of young people today. Still, there are some basic principles that will always be relevant, especially when youth are disenfranchised:

- Supporting communities in speaking for themselves.
- Providing extra attention and funding to young leadership.
- Establishing clear opportunities for connections, mentorship, and inclusion, with strong professional support.
- Listening and respecting the experiences of youth and young adults. Unitarian Univeralist youth and young adults have great strengths today. In growing numbers they have outlined their ideas in clear writings and in relationship with congregations. Their vision for a

just, multicultural, multiracial, intergenerational world is powerful and full of opportunity. We need the wisdom and energy that come from their efforts. Their ideas are seriously tested, their leaders are skilled at negotiating complexity and open to personal transformation, and they enjoy more opportunities to bond with youth in cultures outside their own.

Our racial-justice ideas have been raised and discussed widely through the establishment of Groundwork, the Youth and Young Adult Anti-Racism Training Collective, and a community-wide effort to establish an Anti-Oppression/Anti-Racism Transformation Team that was a top issue for several years at Opus, ConCentric, Con Con and Youth Council. The leaders of youth and young adults have joined together on the issue of racial justice and have worked to support the collective voice of youth and young adults of color. Strategic analysis, training and education, organizing goals, and ethical leadership have been top priorities for nearly eight years. What has emerged is not just one vision, but an understanding that our vision is ultimately dynamic and needs to be held high next to our core mission, as well as continually tested and adjusted, given the new revelations we draw from our experiences. The youth and young adults of today are living out meaningful encounters with identity. They are shaping an identity-positive world. Our young people resist the tendency to deny a person's identity out of fear, power, or ignorance. These efforts are at the core of peacemaking.

X X X

Racial-identity politics in the UUA has advanced to the point that there is finally a level of acceptance of People of Color Ministry and community. The outright rejection and popular attitudes of Eurocentric superiority are in the background now as persons of color have united their voices through DRUUMM (Diverse and Revolutionary Unitarian Universalist Multicultural Ministries), and the intentional development of White Anti-Racist Allies is underway. It has been an intense and difficult struggle, with serious casualties among UU persons of color, particularly African Americans, who have perhaps the longest organized history among people of color in our churches. Nearly 100 ministers and seminarians who identify as people of color are now in regular touch with each other, and out of this milieu come a whole host of deeper and broader questions about the intersection of race and religion in our UU context. Critical thinking around a Unitarian

Universalist people of color ministry is emerging. The Rev. Michelle Bentley has established the Sankofa Project to archive the history of UU people of color, beginning with biographies of religious professionals of color. The Rev. Monica Cummings is preparing an important thesis on pastoral care with UU people of color. I've contributed a history thesis on UU people of color. Our racial-identity questions need more forums for dialogue within our congregations and the UUA, and places for the answers to mature and develop. We must not underestimate the importance or the power of questions that come from within our own underrepresented and traditionally marginalized communities. Authenticity, relevance, and shrewdness come to the fore when a community envisions a more justice-centered and inclusive reality. While in the matter of racial justice, dominant whites need to walk the path of personal realization and adopt institutional transformations, we persons of color *in parallel* need to work collectively and draw on our experiences to signal what meaningful and appropriate change is needed. Whites have the opportunity—and some would say duty—to take responsibility for equality and justice in ways that men, heterosexuals, and able-bodied persons are asked to: emotionally understanding the impact of disparities, socially finding value in equality-in-diversity, and politically supporting efforts to provide equal access and social justice. Without this collective voice, the token voices assume dangerously narrow and potentially self-serving positions of authority. This tendency has long been a destructive habit of Unitarian Universalism, with many good ministers and laypeople of color left suffering in the wake.

Within Unitarian Universalism, what is possible?

- A faith with recognized ministries with people of color in every congregation, UUA district, and Canadian Unitarian Council (CUC) region.

- Cutting-edge knowledge and practices with multiracial-multicultural families and transracial adoptees of color.

- A faith with a permanent commitment to the ministry of people of color, as guided by people of color, and organized through collective groups such as DRUUMM, including an annual general operating grant of at least $125,000 for DRUUMM to be more established in organization, communication, and networking.

- A faith in which every person is made aware of the identity-based ministries offered within congregations, districts, and associations.

- A faith in which every congregation has an active youth ministry and real opportunities are available for youth to meet at the continental level.
- Finally, a faith that continually improves its ability to be justice-making in the context of traditionally marginalized communities, around consciousness-raising, right witness, direct action, and institutional accountability.

Ever since religious professionals of color gathered in Los Gatos, California, to establish DRUUMM in 1997, groups of ten or more people of color have met regularly several times each year. These have been diverse groups in terms of age, racial identity, sexual orientation, and gender. In these spaces, one nagging question has festered unhealthily—our purpose and strategy related to welcoming persons of color into our congregations. The state of affairs has come to the point that folk inside and outside Unitarian Universalism are asking, "Is UU hostile to people of color?" My prayer as a minister is to answer "no," or perhaps "maybe," and to be aware of the efforts to transform hostility into hospitality. Yet I recognize the truth in the experience of conscious, activist, and caring persons of color who engage in the spectrum of church life—from racial-justice to religious-education ministries—who without exception articulate stories of pain and suffering at the hands of our white brothers and sisters and their institutions. Sometimes among people of color we also perpetuate harm on one another, with little energy or support for reconciliation, and undermine our own efforts. Like an addict whose first step to recovery is to name the problem, we need to take the step that study after study has revealed to us: accept that racism is a real, living problem in Unitarian Universalism.

Denial is an issue for every person who lives with privilege. We in our "beloved community" are able to resist this negative behavior to various degrees, yet we still need communities of resistance to support one another. Within the UUA, we are often asked to look at ourselves, our attitudes and practices in relationship to the "other" people of this world, particularly people of color. An institution is designed to protect itself and its image, and thus institutional leaders, both ministers and other professional staff, need to develop an intentional anti-oppression discipline as well as to be held accountable (both privately and publicly) if oppression is to be countered effectively.

Our ability to acknowledge what people of color have been saying within our church walls for generations will allow us to affirm and promote more fully the visions they express. We need to move to this place of strength. Pitfalls abound, particularly our own narcissism. Our habit of overpersonalizing and prioritizing our self-importance at the expense of others fuels a deeply negative attitude toward grassroots racial-justice efforts. We've done well to come off our high horse of paternalistic charity efforts, yet we have a way to go to sustain long-term accountable relationships with communities of color. We expose our weakness in spending more time criticizing the prefix "anti" in anti-racism than in listening to the whole dream of organized people of color and their allies. We signal our opposition when we contradict people who begin to internalize a race-positive view of themselves and the world; for example, when we say, "I don't see race; race isn't real; there is only the human race." We demonstrate our laziness when we fall into the trap of painting anti-racism with one broad brush and not seeing the intense and dynamic diversity in the theology and practice of anti-racist racial-justice ministry.

It has been said that people of color who come to Unitarian Universalism and stay are already experienced at being in a dominant group of whites—and that people of color who have not already adjusted to being in the extreme minority in other settings such as work, school, neighborhood, and so forth rarely make it as a UU in Canadian and American settings. With a few exceptions, the persons of color are from multiracial families with white parents or partners, adoptees of color in otherwise all-white families, or individual well-educated persons of color. Two well-known exceptions are seen in the influx of African Americans who joined urban congregations by the thousands in the 1960s when Unitarian Universalism and particularly large, organized groups of white ministers were seen on the front lines of racial-justice work, and in the groups of refugees given sanctuary in the 1980s, particularly in California congregations.

The evidence and experience suggest that deep hostility toward persons of color still exists in our UU congregations, and that a complicated and persistent racism is at work. The situation has evolved as rapidly as anti-racist efforts have materialized. Ever since the striking 1981 UUA Institutional Racism Audit, serious, long-term, and popular efforts to respond to the shocking realization among white leaders that racism was still an issue in our congregations have been underfunded, have lacked broad religious professional support, and have suffered the dithering of Canadian-American white liberalism. This liberalism continues to obscure our ability to reflect on our own attitudes and behaviors, and minimizes the lived experiences and leadership of others.

We cannot begin to heal and transform our congregations unless we know what needs attention, and unless we are clear about our own vision. The opportunity for assessment and mission development has risen and fallen at the whim of UUA funding and leadership, more recently ebbing without a strong core team. While there have been efforts, including my own in the areas of organizing Seminarians of Color, promoting a program of Anti-Racism Consciousness for Seminarians, and writing a thesis on "Experiences of People of Color in Unitarian Universalism from 1980 to 2005," no active body within the UUA is collecting, analyzing, and reporting on the movement toward anti-racist multiculturalism in a consistent, transparent, and comprehensive way.

As with many injustices, the young people are most at risk. This is where my heart stops as I draw on my own experience as an adoptee of color and realize the massive growth in the number of adoptees in our congregations. If our past behavior is any indicator, without any serious initiative we are condemning the thousands of adopted children of color to a spiritual life that fails to affirm and promote their dignity and worth. What kind of spiritual life will that be? What kind of suffering will this neglect cause? Who has the power to shape a more positive outcome? Important questions remain. Adoptees of color within Unitarian Universalism make up just one microcosm within the communities of color in our congregations. It has been known for over a decade that this group is growing in numbers and is a priority to be addressed. Yet many efforts—multiracial family retreats, workshops, youth of color programs, curriculum and leadership development—have evolved in pockets around the country without the grounding of collective strategic thinking among a broad group of stakeholders. I've been at the center of a number of these projects, co-founding four annual multiracial retreats, co-organizing events and teams of youth and young adults of color. Yet the long-term anti-racist institutionalization has been suppressed, to the detriment of our children. This situation must change, otherwise we will continue to be a church that is 98 percent white.

Change is coming from many directions, and I applaud several of the new efforts by the UUA, including a response to the growing number of seminarians and ministers of color. A serious assessment is being done by Laura Spencer about how to minister to and with youth and young adults of color. People of color continue to meet in large numbers. Yet I believe we need a stronger consensus, a common vision, and theological reflection among the core stakeholders, and the UUA needs to take the lead in facilitating this effort. Even with my insider experience as a former UUA staff member, I do not have access to the broad vision and goals from which we are working and ministering. What is our strategy? How are the various initiatives interconnected? Where can people get more involved? Who is intentionally educating and organizing? How is this effort accountable to the collective experiences of persons of color in Unitarian Universalism?

X   X   X

Young-adult leadership supporting a vision of a just, multiracial, and intergenerational world is in peril. The rapid evolution over the past ten years of organizing young-adult and campus ministry has begun to develop excellent initiatives in the area of theological and spiritual thinking as it relates to Unitarian Universalism and justice issues. Of the 100 people who attended ConCentric 2000 (co-chaired by the now-Rev. Alison Miller and seminarian Rob Keithan, who today is intern minister at First Unitarian in Portland, Oregon), nearly 40 percent of the participants are now ministers or religious professionals—an amazing statistic. The young people—not only from Canada and the United States but also from India, Transylvania, the United Kingdom, and the Philippines—have been connecting with one another and are making significant contributions to Unitarian Universalism. Within our mission to serve congregations, we need this collectivizing of knowledge and action periodically.

The radically inclusive, spiritually alive, and justice-centered theological work that is coming out of young-adult communities is critical to the successful future of Unitarian Universalism. A strong, inclusive, and accountable staff-volunteer body is needed to support our anti-oppression ministries, and particularly our fledgling ministries with people of color. This project needs to be nurtured, funded, staffed, united, and promoted. We need to be linking our efforts together, not segregating them. Professional staff people need to help us interpret, evaluate, and adjust our efforts so that they stay current and effective. Perhaps most important, the grassroots community of leaders from the various sectors of the UUA needs the opportunity to gather every two or three years in the context of a stakeholders' meeting. This last point has been an ongoing top recommendation of the Journey Toward Wholeness Transformation Committee, but it has failed to receive a public response or any action. In this vacuum, activists have come together in smaller numbers for the purposes of sharing, strategic planning, and accountability called for in a stakeholder event, but the withdrawal of UUA support has been devastating for maintaining a shared vision, momentum, and caring for those leading these efforts.

We need continuity, consistency, and comprehensiveness in these ministries. We need to stay in touch with the thinkers and activists, and to allow their work to develop in congregations. We need patience to overcome the natural misunderstandings common in diversity, and patience to work our way into stronger relationships. We need wisdom to be united. The written works and hands-on efforts need to be given opportunities to be shared, with facilitated dialogue and consensus building.

I am a true believer in our faith, and I see much possibility in our efforts to be more truly multiracial and multicultural. I ask every UU to "know thyself." I urge our religious leadership to create literally more opportunities for UU people of color communities to meet. I urge our congregations to inform, invite, and encourage people of color to be connected with such communities. I urge those with the power over our youth and young-adult ministries to expand these efforts, and to build upon the spiritual and justice activism of the last decade.

May we create a better world now, not tomorrow. Let us be awakened! We have the gifts within us and among us. Let us continue to bring them together, and do so intentionally, strategically and consistently.

ONCE IN A LIFETIME: BUILDING INSTITUTIONAL COMMITMENT TO A LIFESPAN UNITARIAN UNIVERSALIST IDENTITY

MICHAEL JAMES TINO

Dan[1] was a fellow guest at the dinner party I was attending while on the road for work. A young man new to the city I was visiting, he was eager to tell his story—of growing up in a Unitarian Universalist congregation, of attending UU camps and conferences as a child and youth, and of realizing his call to do social-justice work full-time after graduating from high school. He told me about a religious educator who meant a great deal to him as a child, a person who turned out to be a friend of mine. I promised to say hello the next time I saw her.

Most of Dan's story was one that made me proud on behalf of all of my colleagues—lay and ordained, paid and volunteer—whose ministry had shaped the life of this wonderful young adult. Then I asked him about his current affiliation with Unitarian Universalism.

"To be honest, I don't feel much like a Unitarian Universalist anymore," he said, the smile disappearing from his face, "I just haven't found anything meaningful in it lately. I guess I'm searching for something that isn't there, and it makes me sad because I've been a UU all my life." I was stunned and dismayed. Unfortunately, Dan's experience is not unique.

The many stories of lifelong Unitarian Universalists who find themselves marginalized in Unitarian Universalist congregations as adults can and should be wake-up calls for our congregations. These stories suggest a need for a serious institutional commitment to understanding Unitarian Universalism as a lifelong faith. Creating this commitment would entail undertaking drastic changes in the practices of our congregations with regard to religious education, worship and leadership development.

Some of these stories come from the intentional efforts of the Unitarian Universalist Association staff to collect the experiences of young adults. In 2006, the UUA Office of Young Adult and Campus Ministry conducted an online survey for self-identified Unitarian Universalists between the ages of 18 and 35. Of the 1,030 respondents, 36.4 percent were not members of Unitarian Universalist congregations, despite their identity as Unitarian Universalists.[2] One of the most striking findings of the survey was that lifelong Unitarian Universalists were *less* likely to be members of congregations than were newer adherents to our faith.

Respondents were asked why they were members of congregations—or why they were not. The free-response answers of the lifelong Unitarian Universalists who remain nonmembers of congregations were fascinating; they serve to underscore some of the institutional gaps our congregations need to address. One young adult who "was raised Unitarian from birth" and was active in youth group, described a lack of connection to worship services:

> When I got out of college I started trying to go to services but I just wasn't into it. The sermons are boring. And I'm not sure I feel a need to be connected to a community like that right now—I have a huge network of friends in my city who are my second family, and I don't need to make friends at church. . . . Going to services just seems kind of lame and doesn't feel like something that has anything to do with me.[3]

Do They Want To Stay?

In her essay in the collection *Essex Conversations: Visions for Lifespan Religious Education*, Judith Frediani paints a bleak picture of the state of our congregations with respect to institutional commitment to a lifespan Unitarian Universalist faith. "The rhetoric of 'lifespan religious education' permeates our publications, brochures and mission statements," she writes. "Yet I am struck by the almost utter failure of the concept to be realized in our denomination."[4] Frediani contrasts the metaphor of the bridge—safely allowing passage over rough transitions in life, and what she posits as desired in our religious communities—with the reality: "a series of bobbing rafts that allow travelers, if they are sufficiently adventurous or persistent, to leap from one to another."[5] Frediani points out that all too often, the system of rafts is itself incomplete, leaving gaps too wide to cross at all. This is a contemptuous way to treat our children.

Some Unitarian Universalists question whether creating a lifespan faith movement is a worthy goal. I contend that many of these questions are so much selfishness cleverly disguised as reasonable arguments. In seeking to justify a condition rightly identified as a problem, these questioners project their own relationship with Unitarian Universalism onto our children and youth. I believe that the goal of a lifespan Unitarian Universalist movement is not only worthy but also completely consistent with the principles that our congregations have covenanted to affirm and promote.

At a recent UUA General Assembly, a delegate declared to me that we should be proud that our children leave our faith. It proves, he argued, that we have given them the self-confidence and reasoning skills to reject what they did not want in their lives.[6] This person sorely misdiagnosed the current state of affairs in our congregations. The vast majority of Unitarian Universalist children who leave our faith as youth and young adults do not disappear as a result of satisfied self-worth and freedom of choice. They do so because they receive the message—explicitly or implicitly—that they are not wanted in our faith community. Our failure to understand this is indicative of the egotism with which many Unitarian Universalists approach a faith that they perceive to be highly individualistic. Thus we conclude, rather glibly, that people are leaving because, well, they want to leave! A careful examination of the reality of our present situation lets us know that this is not the case.

Many people make the case that young people leave our movement because young people, by their very nature, challenge and reject the religion of their upbringing. These perceptions are based partially on an understanding of the developmental stages of life: youth and young adulthood is an intense period of questioning. They are also based partially on many Unitarian Universalists' own experiences of rejecting other faiths as youth and young adults.

In a recent discussion after I preached on this topic, one congregant identified this perception as the source of her own resistance to supporting more youth and young-adult ministry. "I realized listening to you that I've been thinking our youth are going through what I did at that age, when I rejected the Methodist faith of my childhood," she said to me, "Perhaps I should be listening to them instead of making assumptions about what they're going through."[7]

Talking with young people like Dan, it becomes obvious that most Unitarian Universalist young people do not want to leave our faith. They struggle every day to see themselves as Unitarian Universalists despite their lack of connection to Unitarian Universalist institutions. They are glad to have a religious home where their questioning is welcomed as a matter of course. They hunger for spiritual depth and supportive community, yet they do not find what they need in the vast majority of Unitarian Universalist congregations.

One measurable sign that this is the case is the number of people between the ages of 18 and 35 who have signed up as members of the Church of the Younger Fellowship, an online program of the Church of the Larger Fellowship for young adults, since its inception in June of 2005. To date, the congregation-within-a-congregation has signed up more than 500 members in just over two years. There young adults participate in online worship, share joys and concerns and postings to Web logs, form small-group ministry circles, and teach classes for one another. While this virtual congregation is no substitute for the connections built in person (even for this tech-savvy generation), and it is not a multigenerational community, the fact that it is flourishing is a clear sign that young adults seek congregational involvement.

EDUCATION VS. MINISTRY

In examining why youth leave our congregations, we can begin with our literature. From the bookstore of the Unitarian Universalist Association of Congregations, one can buy posters and stickers that claim to put the UUA's principles into language that children can understand. The first principle of our Association is expressed as "each person is important."[8] This is a poor translation, as it misses the notion of *inherence* that makes the first principle unique and revolutionary. Yet many Unitarian Universalist congregations fail to affirm and promote even this simplified children's version when it comes to our youth: young people are routinely given messages that they are not, in fact, important.

Most Unitarian Universalist congregations are heavily invested in educating children. I recently heard colleagues of mine debating whether our congregations do *too* good a job of teaching our children about UU history and world religions. Since most UU adults are not knowledgeable about our history and world religions, my colleagues argued that we may in fact be creating a wider gap between UU youth and UU adults, even discouraging youth from relating to those adults.[9]

It is clear that most children who grow up as Unitarian Universalists have been well educated in our religious education programs. Most can tell us about the seven principles of our Association of Congregations, and most can name a long list of famous Unitarian Universalists from history. Most can talk about holidays celebrated around the world, and a good number have self-worth and decision-making skills around issues of sexuality. Many children who have grown up in our congregations can tell you what worship looks like in the church across town, the synagogue across the street, or the mosque next door—but how many can tell you what worship looks like every Sunday in their own congregation?

Unitarian Universalists in many of our congregations have fundamentally failed to grasp the difference between education and ministry. We educate our children—and we educate them well—but we do not minister to them. In failing to do this, we miss opportunities to let children know that they are, in fact, important to us.

In drawing a distinction between education and ministry, I do not mean in any way to denigrate education as an important part of what we do together as religious communities. Further, I do not mean to imply that education is not an important *part* of ministry. I mean only to say that it is not all there is to ministry. In trying to understand the experience of children in our communities, imagine a congregation whose only programs were adult religious education classes. How many adults would stay in that congregation? Certainly some would, but I don't think the number would be very high.

Education is not all we offer to Unitarian Universalist adults. We offer adults in our congregations ministry. We offer them support through times of crisis and difficulty. We offer them community in which to grow and develop as moral, ethical, and spiritual people. We offer them opportunities and challenges to create a more just society. We offer them worship to help them connect with something greater than themselves—be that God or nature or the power of humanity to change the world around us. When we're living up to our ideals as a faith, we offer our adult members the knowledge that in our congregations, they matter. In building communities based on ministry, we understand that relationships are the core of our faith, and that building relationships with others enriches the whole community.

Children, youth, and young adults need to know that they matter, too. They need to know that they are part of a multigenerational network of relationships that cares about who they are in the present moment as well as in the future. If we really want our children to become Unitarian Universalist adults, we need to begin early sending them the message that they will be supported in our faith. While individual congregations might be engaged in this work, we are not doing this well as a movement. Here is what another young adult—clearly feeling marginalized from the faith tradition she had been taught to claim for her entire life—had to say recently:

> I have been associated with one congregation my whole life, but I don't really have the money or the desire to become an "official" member. Though it is a very large church, I feel that not much is offered for people my age, or at least not much of interest to me. Why support something that doesn't support me?[10]

Ministry to children, youth, and young adults needs to take into account the unique characteristics of life in those age ranges. These three groups of Unitarian Universalists deserve a well-thought-out program of ministry developed with their needs in mind. It is our call as liberal religious people committed to building a strong faith movement to understand what would be the character of that ministry.

What would such a ministry look like? First, it would take professionals who are trained to understand the distinct needs of people in various age groups and developmental stages. Current ministerial education in our movement (both in seminaries and as continuing education) does not adequately deal with the needs of children, youth, and young adults. While some call for the development of specialized professional ministries to children, youth, and young adults, this is an option only for our largest congregations. An understanding of multigenerational ministry must be integrated into the broad training received by all credentialed religious professionals serving our congregations if we are to reach the vast majority of Unitarian Universalists.

Parish ministers must dedicate themselves to engaging with the children and youth in their congregation. This commitment is necessary but not sufficient to provide ministry to children in our congregations. Ministry to and with children should also happen in religious education programs for children. It could, for example, include small-group ministry, such as in the program developed by Gail Forsyth-Vail, director of religious education at North Parish in North Andover, Massachusetts.[11] The Rev. Elizabeth Strong, religious education consultant for the Massachusetts Bay District of the UUA, describes a paradigm shift in congregational programming for children, "from a focus on the information we expect from curriculum to personal spiritual engagement with it."[12]

Ministry to and with youth (as a unique subgroup within our congregations) is currently being explored on an institutional level by our association, and recommendations will be developed at the 2007 Summit on Ministry to and with Youth. One of the most valuable parts of the consultation process leading to the Summit has been the challenge to listen to youth and to take their feedback seriously. As our congregations collect the stories of youth, we will understand more what we need to do to minister to them. As we understand the stories of our youth as part of the overall narrative of our faith, we will hold ourselves accountable to their voices.

LESSONS FROM YOUNG ADULT MINISTRY

By and large, however, the needs of young adults are not a mystery, and what we already know can serve as a starting place for broadening the scope of our ministry. For six years I worked with congregations on improving their ministry to and with young adults. Anecdotal evidence collected from conversations with young adults tells us that most young Unitarian Universalists attend their local congregation at least once in the year following their high-school graduation: their home congregation, a new congregation nearby, or a congregation in a new place of residence.[13] That first year represents a critical transition time in life—and one that congregations ignore at the peril of our entire movement.

The Rev. Marlin Lavanhar, senior minister of All Souls Unitarian Church in Tulsa, Oklahoma, in an interview for the UUA-produced film *Campus Ministry: Building Intergenerational Wholeness*, reflected on the critical role of faith communities in the young adult years:

> We probably confront five of the eight most important decisions we're ever going to make in our entire lives: questions about sexuality, questions about jobs and careers, questions about joining the military or not joining the military . . . having a family, having a child . . . all those things are questions that most people confront between the ages of 18 and their early thirties. It's probably the most important time for there to be a church community, a net of people of different ages . . . that you can count on. . . .[14]

Sharon Daloz Parks, through her studies of young-adult spirituality and faith development, contends that the "big questions" being answered in the young-adult years "are religious questions because they touch the whole of life."[15] They cannot be answered in isolation, and take mentoring and guidance from those who have been there before. Communities of faith are uniquely positioned to be the multigenerational context in which young-adult questions can find their religious home.

UUA President William Sinkford connects this need directly to the principles that Unitarian Universalist congregations have covenanted to affirm and promote. "It's hard to claim that you're interested in the responsible search for truth and meaning and not be interested in persons who are in their most intense period of that search for truth and meaning," he said in an interview. "I actually don't have much patience with folks who don't understand their Unitarian Universalism to call them to reach out to all people."[16]

Congregations can and should be developing plans for the inclusion of young adults in their ministry. This effort involves getting to know young people, understanding their history with our faith, and inviting them to be an active part of the shared ministry of our congregations. Since a primary goal of young-adult ministry is the faith development of young adults themselves, that development must be planned in accountable and authentic relationship with young adults. Parks notes that "the religious community does not fulfill its role in the formation of young adult faith unless it can recognize the gifts of young adults, welcome their emerging competence, and give them power."[17] Young adults should be given permission and responsibility to help shape the ministry of Unitarian Universalist congregations that seek to include them.

MINISTRY AND MEMBERSHIP: EXAMINING POLICIES AND PRACTICES

Discussions of inclusion and ministry invariably lead to a consideration of congregational membership, since our movement is based on congregational polity and values the role of the individual within our congregational communities. The commitment of membership is a vital one in developing strong Unitarian Universalist institutions, and needs to be accompanied by certain responsibilities on the part of the member. "Of course," writes Judith Frediani, "to make meaning of our lives in religious community, we have to show up."[18] Congregational membership—and the attendant commitment to show up as a member—must be open and accessible to young adults. This inclusion involves changing attitudes, policies and practices currently in place in many of our congregations.

One potential set of stumbling blocks to young-adult membership in Unitarian Universalist congregations has to do with congregational attitudes and assumptions about young adults. Often the assumption is made that young people new to our congregations are also new to our faith. Our faith is often described as one for people coming from other faith traditions. This description does a grave disservice to lifelong Unitarian Universalists, explains the Rev. Barbara Wells ten Hove:

> For a long time I have been asking myself why I am still an active and committed Unitarian Universalist. Too often in UU settings, I feel like a stranger in my own hometown.
>
> Some years ago, during General Assembly, I had an experience that disturbed me. A minister leading a program asked people to raise their hands if they were raised Catholic. A good number of hands in the room went up. Then he asked, How many were raised Jewish? Muslim? Protestant? Unchurched? How about fundamentalist Christian? Then he asked, How many have been a UU for ten to twenty years? Five to ten years? Less than five years? Less than one year?
>
> After he had finished, he happily acknowledged the diversity in the room. But I felt angry and frustrated. None of those categories fit me. He had forgotten or ignored those of us adults who were born and raised in our denomination. What we call "home-bred" Unitarian Universalists may be rare birds, but we are not extinct.[19]

If we are committed to building a Unitarian Universalist movement based on lifelong commitments to our faith, we cannot continue to marginalize those who have been born into it (or brought in as children). Few young people whose experiences are not valued will stick around; fewer still will become ministers in our movement, able to share their experiences.

We must also unearth and discard policies and practices that reinforce false assumptions about youth and young adults in our congregations. As another young adult wrote in a response to the UUA's survey:

> Although I was dedicated a UU baby, raised in the church, [and] attended Sunday school every day of every year until I graduated from high school, my congregation does not allow me to become a member until I go through the "traditional" path of membership, i.e., a "What is Unitarian Universalism?" class.... I feel that my 23 years as a UU should qualify as enough but my congregation does not feel the same.[20]

There is no reason why our congregational membership policies cannot be written to accommodate long-time Unitarian Universalists seeking to formalize their relationship with our faith. We would probably make an exception to policies like the one described above for someone moving to town having been an adult member in another congregation—why are we so hesitant to do the same for those who were children among us?

In examining our membership policies with regard to youth and young adults, we are led to examine our entire membership program—and indeed, larger cultural issues at work in our congregations. We might ask ourselves: How do we welcome people into our congregations? How do we connect them to our communities? How do we encourage people to stay? Building an institutional structure that encourages people to develop lifelong commitments to our faith means creating a culture in which people stick around through tough times. It means creating a covenant that holds fast through conflicts and stresses. It means understanding privilege and entitlement and overcoming rampant individualism. It means making a commitment to one another and inviting others into that commitment.

Next, we must as a faith examine our practices of stewardship and pledging. Many young adults cite expectations in regard to financial giving as a significant obstacle to congregational membership.[21] In discussing the matter with young adults, I have found that while young adults are willing to be generous with institutions they support, talk of large amounts of money turns them off. In addition, it is not only young people who are made to feel guilty when they cannot afford the amounts cited as "the average pledge we need from our members" when such language is used.

It is not only from young adults that we hear the call to shift our language about giving and congregational stewardship from one of amount to one of generosity as a spiritual practice. This shift allows people to feel comfortable developing generous giving habits, and encourages congregations to move to an assumption of abundance. As in modern interpretations of the biblical miracle of the loaves and fishes, I believe that the practice of generosity uncovers the abundance that has been there all along. It feeds the masses despite the voices of naysayers and those who insist on a culture of scarcity. Generosity is a practice that creates rewards in our lives—the rewards of abundance, of goodwill, of compassion, and of being able to live the values we claim.

Young people hearing a message about the value of generosity are more likely to make the commitment of membership. Further, asking for a commitment to generosity in the present will lead to larger contributions in the future, when careers and families are more established. While students and young adults beginning their careers might not be able to make large donations, a focus on generosity gives them the incentive to get there. The congregation of which I was a member for many years did just this, and by the age of 29, my giving level (5 percent of my professional salary) qualified me as a "major donor" to the congregation.

PROGRAMS AND POSSIBILITIES

Our congregations' programs also need to be rethought using the lens of multigenerational community. One example of a program ready for a multigenerational approach in many congregations is the social-justice emphasis. Unitarian Universalist youth and young adults have been challenging older adults in our movement for several years around issues of justice-making and anti-racism, anti-oppression, and multiculturalism. These challenges call us back to our Universalist roots in advocating a ministry in which all people are treated as equally loved.

It is clear from listening to youth and young adults that Unitarian Universalist congregations are not living up to their ideals with respect to anti-oppression, anti-racism, and multiculturalism. As institutions in a world set up to favor certain groups, our congregations have systems of oppression at their core. This is not to say that congregations are evil institutions, but that any institution not specifically set up to oppose the status quo of oppression in our society winds up participating in those systems.

To understand this concept, one might witness the classism that surfaces in so many pledge campaigns when people are asked to aim for an "average" pledge. Or perhaps one could consider the racism inherent in the different treatment of newcomers to our congregations based on their skin color: several Unitarian Universalist friends of color have reported to me incidents in which they were instantly told about the Christian church down the street; I have never heard such an anecdote from a white person.[22] One might also examine the facilities of a congregation from the perspective of someone who uses a wheelchair or has other severe mobility restrictions to understand how ableism is often kept in check only by building codes.

That these things are engrained in our systems makes the work that much harder. Because we are dealing with institutionalized systems of oppression, we need to create institutional, systemic responses. Creating lasting culture change is more difficult than changing individual attitudes, and many of our congregations stop doing this work when it gets too hard. To make Unitarian Universalism a lifelong faith, however, we must respond to the challenges our young people give us in regard to anti-oppression work.

For many of these young people our anti-oppression work is not a theoretical construct—it is based in their direct experience of the world.

Because of the high incidence of transracial adoption (including the fact that it has been popular of late for upper-middle-class American families to adopt children from Asia and Latin America) and the growing number of multiracial families, there are many more children of color in our congregations than adults of color. Because we teach our children to be open and honest about their gender and sexuality, many lesbian, gay, bisexual, and transgender people are "coming out" as youth—many more than did just 10 or 20 years ago.

Further, because we teach our children well, even those who identify as heterosexual and white often have acute sensitivity to the experiences of their peers who are different from them. We teach our children that "every person is important"; as youth and young adults, they expect us to live up to this ideal. We should be neither surprised nor upset by this expectation.

And yet, we fall short. We fall short in understanding the dynamics of race, class, sexual orientation, gender, and other identities in our society. In doing so, we wind up creating religious institutions that mirror systems of oppression—racism, classism, heterosexism, sexism, etc.—and make people with marginalized identities feel unsafe. This reality is noticed. Another young adult, responding to the UUA survey, connected this lack of safety to her own desire to be a part of our congregations:

> Many of my friends of color and trans[gender and] genderqueer friends
> don't feel safe in congregations and I can't in good conscience participate
> in a congregation or congregational institutions that make my friends
> and loved ones feel unsafe.[23]

To our young people, this work is about their friends. It is about their peers. It is about those with whom they have direct personal connection. They see issues of anti-racism and anti-oppression as basic issues of inclusion and relationship. To youth and young adults, anti-racism and anti-oppression are profoundly theological matters—based on theologies that prefer a communal, rather than an individualistic, approach to religion. It is time for Unitarian Universalist adults, especially our religious professionals, to come to this realization as well.

TOUCHING THE THIRD RAIL: WORSHIP

There is, of course, one program in our congregations in which change invariably results in a strong reaction. The final and most important obstacle to the ongoing participation of children, youth and young adults in Unitarian Universalist congregations is the very feature that brings most of us together: worship. Sunday-morning worship needs to be made more hospitable across generations without making it irrelevant to those seeking an intellectually rigorous and meaningful faith.

Three factors make this an important and dangerous topic. First, as mentioned earlier, children and youth rarely experience Sunday-morning worship in Unitarian Universalist congregations; when they do, it is usually an "intergenerational" service that serves neither adults nor children particularly well. Second, the experiences youth have with worship are profoundly different from the corporate worship in our congregations. Third, there is in many congregations a reluctance to revisit forms of worship that are regarded as having become stale and outdated, leaving many of us with worship that is unwelcoming to all but a select few.

Most Sunday-morning worship services in Unitarian Universalist congregations are patently unwelcoming to children and youth. In many of our congregations, we admit as much explicitly. The congregation I serve as minister once wrote on its website for newcomers, "We frequently have children staying in the adult service, although some find it boring after a while."[24] That we separate our worship experience into the "adult service" and "other" is a clear indication that Sunday worship is not meant for a multigenerational congregation.

When Unitarian Universalist congregations do schedule a "special" intergenerational service, it is often either a service for adults that children are forced to sit through or a service for children that is boring to adults. A growing number of Unitarian Universalist ministers are exploring ways to develop multigenerational worship—worship that is open and accessible to all people, whatever their age. In doing so, they are creating worship that connects with people on multiple levels, including *both* intellectual stimulation and simple messages that children can understand. The Rev. Greg Ward, former minister of the Unitarian Universalist Metro Atlanta North congregation, creates such worship. While he was serving as minister there, the congregation quoted his philosophy of worship on its website (in a section written as an interview with him by an unnamed web author):

> There is a very creative element within the ministry here at UUMAN. That is something that is really appreciated here. We understand that when there are many different truths which undergird our lives, we must reach out to them and celebrate them in a myriad of ways. I love the freedom of the church and the excitement with which everyone participates. In this place, there are very few spectators. We're all participants."[25]

The Rev. Erika Hewitt of the Live Oak Unitarian Universalist Congregation in Goleta, California, is another minister exploring what it means to welcome people of all ages into worship on Sunday mornings. She does this using a model she calls "spirited worship," which she describes as "services that are interactive, high-energy, and creative. Spirited worship offers people a chance to connect across the generations, and invites everyone to share experiences of awe, amusement, celebration, grief, gratitude, and questioning."

Other models for vibrant, meaningful multigenerational worship surely exist. More attention needs to be paid to what it means to design and lead worship for a multigenerational congregation. Ministerial training can and should also take this concern into account.

Another major barrier to the inclusion of youth in Sunday-morning worship services is the stark difference between the experiences of worship that youth have on a regular basis and what Unitarian Universalist congregations offer on Sunday morning. There is little understanding among youth (and scarcely more among ministers) that the purposes of congregational worship on Sunday morning and the "circle worship" found in youth community are completely different. To youth, worship is an intimate time for sharing and exploration. Often conducted in a circle, youth worship goes very deep, very quickly. This model, of course, is unsuitable for use in a worship service designed to be open and welcoming.

There are two things (at least) that need to be done to address this. First, youth, when introduced to the circle worship format, must be educated as to its benefits and limitations. They must know that building intimacy through worship is not the function of congregational worship, and they must understand that their own worship is not designed to welcome newcomers (rather, it is designed to increase the bonds of an already-formed group). Youth are regularly trained to prepare worship through such programs as Spirituality Development Conferences offered by the UUA. This training must include a discussion of the purposes of worship and the different ways to achieve those purposes. It must analyze ways in which group intimacy is built, and it must unpack the responsibility of our youth groups to be hospitable places.

Second, Unitarian Universalist congregations must develop appropriate ways to develop intimacy in their communities. It is telling that our youth miss the deep bonds created during circle worship when they become adults trying to find their place in Unitarian Universalist congregations. These bonds—not appropriately created in worship—must be created somewhere.

The best programs to encourage such bonds are small-group ministry or covenant-group programs. Small-group ministry programs have several aspects that appeal to those seeking to create multigenerational community. I believe that they hold special promise for those seeking to include people who have grown up in Unitarian Universalist youth communities in our congregations.

Covenant groups are based on caring, listening and respect. Group rules allow everyone to talk and ask everyone to listen. Members get to know one another and form a deep community, allowing them to care for each other even outside the group. Small groups are flexible and responsive to the needs of their members. Covenant groups also foster closeness that is unavailable or uncomfortable in larger groups. They offer a way to build community bonds with people with whom you might not have a lot else in common. They allow their members to share at progressively deeper levels, creating intimacy based in mutual ties to the group.

Covenant groups are more than social groups and different from corporate worship experiences. Their most important goal is the spiritual growth of their members, and the covenant is written to provide a safe space for that growth. That space is sacred space—space designated as special and unique. On the other hand, covenant groups must, by their design, open themselves up to newcomers from time to time, making sure that they don't become social cliques.

Perhaps most important, small groups offer something familiar to the common experiences of many youth. People who have been a part of a Unitarian Universalist youth group know the importance of "touch groups" at youth conferences. Touch groups allow people to touch base with one another amid the hustle and bustle and mega-community-building that goes on at these gatherings. Covenant groups offer a similar experience—and can be considered touch groups on life. They also have the sharing component so essential to youth circle worship, allowing multiple voices to be heard and relationships to be made.

Finally, in many UU congregations there is significant resistance—on the part of both ministers and laypeople—to a thorough analysis of worship practices with an eye to updating outdated rituals and forms. Unfortunately, this resistance only serves to stifle change and innovation in our worship, and to turn off those who approach things differently from our current worship planners. Many of those turned off by outdated forms of worship are young people eager to embrace a more contemporary approach.

Resistance to worship labeled as "contemporary" is often based in faulty assumptions. For example, too often people assume that to be contemporary, worship needs to be intellectually simple, performed at high volume, and openly theist. None of these need be the case.

In early 2007, I had the opportunity to organize a conference on contemporary worship in Unitarian Universalist congregations. This conference had as its goal not the imposition of a new model of worship, but rather the open exchange of ideas on how to make Unitarian Universalist worship "spiritually vital and alive." I invited presenters with a wide variety of experience, and registration was open to all, so the conference included seminarians, ministers, religious educators, music professionals, and lay leaders.

In the discussions about what made worship "contemporary," patterns emerged. One of the most obvious patterns focused our concept of intelligence (and intellectual rigor) in worship. Time and again, participants and presenters talked about engaging multiple intelligences in worship,[26] including visual, musical, interpersonal, kinesthetic, and spatial elements, in addition to the ways in which we ask people to listen and comprehend speech. In taking into account multiple-intelligence theory in designing worship, ministers would make their already intellectually rigorous worship service available to a broader range of people, including younger people seeking our faith communities.

It is clear that our worship should be open to adaptation and change. Such openness would require leadership by ministers trained in the theory as well as the practice of worship. Seminary education would need to involve work on multiple intelligences and an understanding of what they mean outside the classroom setting. Laypeople in our congregations would need to be open to the evolution of worship forms. As we know, change inevitably brings anxiety, and anxiety needs to be managed.

Concluding Thoughts

Dan's story of finding his spiritual needs unmet in Unitarian Universalist congregations should be rare. Rather, it is a commonplace occurrence in our congregations: young people who have spent all their growing-up years among us feel disconnected from our faith movement once they become adults. We can reach all of our members through an institutional commitment to multigenerational *ministry*: a ministry that lets people of all ages know that they matter. We must make Unitarian Universalist practices—worship, education, justice-making—available to Unitarian Universalists of all ages. Then our congregations will be places in which to spend a lifetime.

NOTES

1. Not his real name. Dan's story, however, is real, and based on an informal conversation—not a formal interview. Thus, I have changed some of the details to protect his privacy.

2. UUA Office of Young Adult and Campus Ministry, *2006 Survey of Unitarian Universalist Young Adults* (Boston: Unitarian Universalist Association of Congregations [internal document]), 2006.

3. Anonymous response, *2006 Survey of Unitarian Universalist Young Adults.*

4. Judith Frediani, "Making Sure There Is a There There" in *Essex Conversations: Visions for Lifespan Religious Education* (Boston: Skinner House Press, 2001), p. 56.

5. Frediani, p. 56.

6. From a direct conversation with a delegate to the 2005 General Assembly in Fort Worth, Texas. I did not record the delegate's name at the time.

7. Pamela DiLavore, personal communication with author.

8. "Children's Principles" materials (Boston: Unitarian Universalist Association). Available at UUA bookstore as of 12/10/06.

9. From a private discussion among several UU seminarians, some of whom were professional religious educators, some of whom grew up UU, and some of whom were raising UU children.

10. Anonymous response, *2006 Survey of Unitarian Universalist Young Adults.*

11. *See* Gail Forsyth-Vail, *Adapting Small Group Ministry for Children's Religious Education,* vol. 1 and 2 (North Andover, Mass.: North Parish, Unitarian Universalist, 2003 and 2006, respectively).

12. The Rev. Elizabeth M. Strong, as quoted on the UUA website for UUA General Assembly 2003, *New Paradigms in Lifespan Faith Development: http://www.uua.org/ga/ga03/0304.html* (link active as of 1/16/07).

13. Joseph Santos-Lyons (UUA director of Campus Ministry and Field Organizing), personal correspondence with author.

14. Interview with the Rev. Marlin Lavanhar conducted by Benjamin Ernst, in *Campus Ministry: Building Intergenerational Wholeness.* Film produced by the Unitarian Universalist Association, Boston, 2002.

15. Sharon Daloz Parks, *Big Questions, Worthy Dreams: Mentoring Young Adults in Their Search for Meaning, Purpose and Faith* (San Francisco: Jossey-Bass, 2000), p. 198.

16. Interview with the Rev. William Sinkford conducted by Benjamin Ernst in *Campus Ministry: Building Intergenerational Wholeness.*

17. Parks, p. 203.

18. Frediani, p. 54.

19. Barbara Wells ten Hove, "A Stranger in My Hometown," *UU World,* spring 2006.

20. Anonymous response, *2006 Survey of Unitarian Universalist Young Adults.*

21. *2006 Survey of Unitarian Universalist Young Adults.*

22. Elandria Williams, personal conversation with author.

23. Anonymous response, *2006 Survey of Unitarian Universalist Young Adults.*

24. Unitarian Universalist Fellowship of Northern Westchester, website *www. uufellowship.org.* Such language is no longer found on this website.

25. Unitarian Universalist Metro Atlanta North, website, "Our Minister, Rev. Greg Ward," found online at *http:www.uman.org/* (link valid as of 4/27/07).

26. See the work of Dr. Howard Gardner and his followers, including *Frames of Mind: The Theory of Multiple Intelligences* (New York: Basic Books, 1983); *Multiple Intelligences: The Theory in Practice* (New York: Basic Books, 1993); and *Intelligence Reframed: Multiple Intelligences for the 21st Century* (New York: Basic Books, 2000).

BIOGRAPHICAL NOTES

ERIK DAVID CARLSON is a student at Meadville Lombard Theological School in Chicago; a co-recipient of the UUA Donna DiSciullo Award for Young Adult and Campus Ministry with business partner Jonathan Craig; a member of the Church of the Younger Fellowship Web Team, and cofounder of Revolution Media (http://revolution.com), a company dedicated to providing technology solutions to Unitarian Universalist organizations and societies. Erik is spending the 2007–2008 academic year on internship working with the three New Orleans-area churches in ministry, pastoral counseling and technological outreach. He is recording his experiences in New Orleans on his personal blog available at *http://ErikDavid.com.*

THE REV. JENNIFER CROW lives in Rochester, New York, with her partner, Loretta Mitchell. She serves the First Unitarian Church of Rochester as associate minister, with a focus on pastoral care, innovative adult spiritual development programming, and youth work. She believes that innovation and tradition are the foundation of our constantly emerging church.

THE REV. JOHN CULLINAN serves as minister of the Unitarian Church in Los Alamos, New Mexico. He lives in Los Alamos with his wife, Jess, and their two children. He is a graduate of Meadville Lombard Theological School in Chicago and holds a B.A. from Marquette University in Milwaukee, Wisconsin.

THE REV. MARLIN LAVANHAR is the senior minister of All Souls Unitarian Church in Tulsa, Oklahoma. Marlin grew up a Unitarian Universalist in Illinois. He majored in sociology at Tulane University and graduated from Harvard Divinity School. When he was called to All Souls in 2000 at age 32, he became the youngest person to serve as senior minister of a major congregation in the denomination. Before serving at All Souls, Marlin was assistant minister at the First and Second Church of Boston. Marlin is also the creator of the Soulful Sundown model of contemporary worship.

THE REV. TAMARA LEBAK is the assistant minister at All Souls Unitarian Church in Tulsa, Oklahoma, and is an independent organizational consultant and executive coach. In her ministry as well as in her consulting, Tamara integrates her training in Gestalt Organization and Systems Development, conflict management, appreciative inquiry, and community organizing in diverse racial and economic settings. Tamara has worked with numerous educational, religious, community and nonprofit institutions, including the National Park Service and the World Bank. She has been a chaplain at a maximum-security prison and a university hospital, and a French and epistemology teacher and a certified Community Leader of Qigong.

THE REV. BRET LORTIE is the senior minister at First Unitarian Universalist Church, San Antonio, Texas. In his former career as a writer and journalist, he served as managing editor for *The Bulletin of the Atomic Scientists*, a peace magazine dedicated to the nonproliferation of nuclear weapons and arms control. He plays trombone, guitar, and various other musical instruments.

THE REV. SHANA LYNNGOOD serves as the associate minister of All Souls Church, Unitarian, in Washington, D.C. She shares her life with her partner, the Rev. Melora Lynngood, and their daughter, Athena. In addition to ministry, Shana is passionate about jazz, art, and poetry.

THE REV. NANCY MCDONALD LADD has served the Bull Run Unitarian Universalist Congregation in Manassas, Virginia, since 2004. She is a graduate of Meadville Lombard Theological School in Chicago. During seminary, she served as intern minister at the Unitarian Universalist Church in Rockford, Illinois, and sabbatical minister at the Universalist Unitarian Church in Joliet, Illinois. Nancy currently serves on the Executive Committee of the Chesapeake Area UU Ministers' Association.

THE REV. JOSH PAWELEK serves as parish minister of the Unitarian Universalist Society, East, in Manchester, Connecticut. He also serves as a leader in a variety of justice-making organizations in Connecticut, including the Greater Hartford Interfaith Coalition for Equity and Justice, Congregations United For Racial Equality and Justice, and Connecticut Clergy for Marriage Equality. He lives in Glastonbury, Connecticut, with his wife, Stephany Pascetta, and their two young sons, Mason and Max.

DAVID PYLE is a chaplain in the U.S. Army, as well as a former enlisted Army intelligence analyst. He is a Master of Divinity student at the Meadville Lombard Theological School in Chicago, a member of the Church of the Larger Fellowship, an associate member of the UU Fellowship of Galveston County, Texas, and a member of the Empty Sound Zen Temple in Oak Park, Illinois. David is the co-founder of the Great Lakes Military Ministry Project and the coordinator of UU Military Ministries and the "UUs in the Military" Web forum. David served on the UUA Task Force that redrafted the UUA policies on military and federal chaplaincy endorsement. He holds a bachelor's degree in history and political science from East Tennessee State University.

SHERI REDA is a writer, editor, performer, and educator with more than 25 years experience in professional publishing and nearly as many years in theater. She was the founding editor of *Conscious Choice* magazine and has written textbooks and articles on topics related to English, theater, speech, religion, and social studies. After graduating from Meadville Lombard Theological Seminary in Chicago in 2006, she began using her professional work to explore the intersection of faith and action.

THE REV. JOSEPH SANTOS-LYONS was raised in the West Hills Unitarian Universalist Fellowship in Portland, Oregon. A domestic adoptee of Chinese and Czech descent, Joseph has long been engaged with issues of racial justice and involved in various people of color communities. He lives with his partner and their three children.

THE REV. KRISTA TAVES is the settled minister of Emerson Unitarian Universalist Chapel, Ellisville, Missouri. She has served as interim minister of First Unitarian Universalist Church of New Orleans and First Unitarian Universalist Church of Springfield, Missouri; ministerial leader of the Unitarian Fellowship of Northwest Toronto; and consulting minister of the Unitarian Congregation of Guelph, Ontario. Before entering the ministry Krista pursued graduate studies in Canadian religious and cultural history at York University in Toronto and devoted herself to laying the foundations for an organized bisexual community in Toronto.

DR. MICHAEL TINO is a newly-fellowshipped Unitarian Universalist minister who has been director of Young Adult and Campus Ministry for the Unitarian Universalist Association of Congregations since 2001. Michael is a 2007 graduate of Meadville Lombard Theological School in Chicago; he also holds a Ph.D. from Duke University. He lives in Durham, North Carolina, with his partner, Eric, and is a member of the Church of the Younger Fellowship, a subsidiary of the Church of the Larger Fellowship.

ALL SOULS
UNITARIAN CHURCH

2952 S Peoria, Tulsa, OK 74114 ~ 1-800-588-2601
or fax 918-743-0518 ~ www.AllSoulsChurch.org

Name:

Street Address:

City, State, Zip:

Phone:

E-Mail:

Item	Quantity	Unit Price	Total Price
Rev. X (book)*			
Living the Call (book)*		See Below	
The Almost Church (book)*			
The Gift of Doubt (book)*			
Our American Roots - DVD		$75.00	
Our American Roots - VHS		$65.00	
Simple Gifts, Too - note cards (10 count, blank inside)		$12.00	
Simple Gifts, Too - poster		$20.00	
Simple Gifts, Too - CD-ROM		$25.00	
Simple Gifts, Too - poster (signed)		$65.00	
Simple Gifts, Too - giclée* (shipping $40 ea.)		$750.00	

Book Quantity Pricing		Postage Rates	Subtotal	
1-5	$14.00 ea.		Book Postage	
6-10	$12.00 ea.	Call or e-mail for rates	Other Postage	
11-30	$10.00 ea.			
			Total Order	

Payment Method: □ Check   □ Mastercard   □ VISA
Card Account Number:

| | | | | | | | | | | | | | | | | | | | | | | | |

3 digit code

| | | | | | |

Expiration Date

_____
Signature of Authorized Buyer

_____
Print Name Clearly

Books are sent USPS media mail in the United States; for expedited shipping rates, quantities larger than 30, or international shipping rates please contact All Souls at the above numbers.